Advance Praise

"Shirley M. Phillips' memoir is a story of breaking barriers and persistence in being taken seriously as a pilot and a mother of a child with disabilities. Her experiences as one of few female pilots honed the advocacy skills needed to ensure the medical field took her daughter's, and later her own, health care needs seriously. Phillips uses humor to help us grapple with weighty issues. She reminds us to trust our 'gut' when facing challenging situations. Truly an inspirational story of courage and perseverance against the odds."

— Laurie L. Gordy, PhD, Higher Education Administrator

"*How Not to Fly an Airplane* is an exhilarating book that reveals the joys and challenges of being an early female pilot for a major airline, teaching aviation to college students, and balancing motherhood. Phillips shares her experiences as a child model with her identical twin sister, her flying lessons at the age of fourteen, piloting scenic flights during her college days, and the two engine failures that she experienced before she even turned twenty-six. The book is a memoir of her career and personal life, filled with white-knuckle moments and twists and turns."

— Kathleen Fitzpatrick, Professor of History

"In this engaging memoir, Shirley's journey as a pioneering female pilot is both inspiring and heartfelt. The stories of her overcoming resistance from male colleagues, who doubted her abilities simply because of her gender, are empowering and relatable for women in male-dominated fields. Her reflections on downplaying femininity to fit into a masculine culture resonate deeply with my own experiences in the industry. The emotional depth of her family life, particularly the medical struggles of one daughter and the loving care by the other, brings a personal touch to her professional triumphs. Shirley's writing strikes the perfect balance, offering enough detail to captivate readers without getting lost in nuance. This book is not only entertaining and uplifting but should be on everyone's must-read list."

— Kimberly Perkins, PhD, B787 Airline Pilot

How Not to Fly an Airplane

How Not to Fly an Airplane

A Female Pilot's Journey

Shirley M. Phillips

Copyright © 2025 by Shirley M. Phillips

All rights reserved. No part of this book may be reproduced or transmitted in any form or by any means, electronic or mechanical, including photocopy, recording, or any information storage and retrieval system, without prior permission from the publisher (except by reviewers who may quote brief passages).

Many names of the people that are the subjects of essays in this memoir have been changed to protect their privacy. All the stories are true to the best of my memory.

First Edition

Caseback ISBN: 978-1-62720-590-0
Paperback ISBN: 978-1-62720-591-7
Ebook ISBN: 978-1-62720-592-4

Design by Molly Gerard
Editorial Development by Grace Gilrane
Promotional Development by Emily Metheny

Published by Apprentice House Press

Apprentice House Press
Loyola University Maryland

Loyola University Maryland
4501 N. Charles Street, Baltimore, MD 21210
410.617.5265
www.ApprenticeHouse.com
info@ApprenticeHouse.com

For my father who started it all, and my daughters Christina and Ashley. For all the pilots who shared the skies with me.

Contents

Foreword xi
The Making of a Flight Instructor 1
Twins 13
Checkrides 21
My First Day as a Professional Pilot 35
Unable 41
Baby Bumps 49
From the Cockpit to the Cadaver 67
How to Not Fly an Airbus 79
Grounded 95
Air Rage 109
Too Close to Home 113
Mayday 121
Teaching Dad 137
One of the Guys 143
How Not to Fly an Airplane 157
He Was a Hero, She Was Calm 165
Before and After Pete 175
Who is Your Captain 187
My Second Engine Failure 193
She is a Pilot 199
Acknowledgments 205
Prior Publications 207
About the Author 209
Glossary 211

Foreword

For anyone who's not a pilot, who has sipped a to-go container of overpriced coffee and pinched a carry-on with their knees at a departure gate while observing the flight crew roll their own carry-ons down the polished floor of the airport terminal, anyone like me, this book by Shirley Phillips explains a few things. The matching dark suits on two men, usually men, headed to their next flight assignment, hotel accommodations, or perhaps to a parking garage and homeward. Playing the guessing game of who's captain and who's co-pilot, the hierarchy usually whiffable. What does Phillips' book confirm? That the aviation industry as an employer, as a profession, is rife with complications, disparities, and unfairness—along with the sheer joy of flight, comradery, and accomplishment. That some pilots must overcome or at best navigate the disparities behind those uniforms, the interpersonal messiness that happens in a shut cockpit.

For these readers, Shirley Phillips' *How Not to Fly an Airplane: A Female Pilot's Journey* functions like Anthony Bourdain's *Kitchen Confidential*. This book could do what Bourdain's did to the restaurant industry—which exposed the brutal working conditions of chefs and kitchen workers, warning diners off ordering fish from the menu on Monday—except here it's the transportation industry and the potential consequences for the flying customer.

For pilots reading this book, it will likely be refreshing to see a fellow pilot speak freely about what occurs on-the-job. Phillips' experience as a flight instructor and pilot might be the pilot-reader's experience, unspoken. "This is your captain speaking": but who is *not* usually allowed to speak their mind? Whose professional opinion has been overruled? Whose career was roadblocked by sexism, where pregnancy might be a liability, where of eighty professionals, only six are women, as was the case with Phillips early in her career?

Phillips is an adroit storyteller. Each chapter provides a satisfying narrative arc. What's at stake is patently clear to professional and non-professional aviation audiences (not an easy feat for writers). Phillips makes the central concerns of the profession understandable to outsiders; she is clearly a natural born teacher. She offers memorable examples of near accidents and actual fatalities. As someone who has survived not one but two engine failures, and who laments those who did not survive aviation incidents (including former students), her authority is riveting.

Through storytelling, Phillips shares with us what it's like to give flying lessons to one's own father or nearly crash with her twin sister as a passenger. How she once used her "therapeutic voice" with a student whose personality transforms in the no-exit space of a cockpit and who reveals to her that he had killed someone. She describes how a pilot makes such a bad decision that a flight attendant quits after the flight and takes a bus home (not a plane): the equivalent of a line chef in Anthony Bourdain's world refusing to eat at a Michelin Star restaurant where she works and heading to Burger King instead, serious warning bells. Only what could happen is a lot worse than a case of food poisoning. Phillips tells what it was like to be selected to train for the prestigious Airbus in August 2001, only to be laid-off along with the other simulator trainees and then transition to a career at an aviation college.

Phillips vividly describes the people in her professional and personal circles. Normal, on-the-ground interpersonal relationships are more intense in the confined setting of a cockpit, in a high-stakes situation in which one's own life and the lives of passengers and crew are in the balance from moment to moment, literally removed from the ordinary workings of the planet surface yet controlled by FAA regulations and air traffic control like a sort of omniscient narrator. The plot lines of these chapters take concerns of the aviation profession—situational awareness, avoiding confirmation bias, cockpit resource management—and make them fundamental human interaction.

For any of us who've looked up at tiny planes in the sky and wondered what it might be like to teach others to fly, to have one's safety bound to the varying ability of one's students, Phillips details in slow-motion those seconds in which every decision as the leader is lifesaving or life-taking.

Once, in the cockpit with an oblivious mentee, Phillips found herself in a dangerous spin, as described in the book's opening pages:

"It had the aura of an out of body experience as I watched an apple orchard directly below us grow bigger through the big glass canopy." *How Not to Fly an Airplane* comes with many moments of humor, too. Humor is part of leading younger professionals toward their best lives as pilots. Phillips describes planting issues like Easter eggs to be discovered by novice pilots but then, like a parent hiding actual plastic Easter eggs, needing to remember exactly how many issues were left to be discovered after the "hunt" was completed and where to find the ones still hidden.

Phillips demonstrates what it takes to speak up when something is direly wrong, despite the personal consequences. As she says, "[M]y responsibility was to the passengers—not worrying about being well-liked. A lot of well-liked pilots were dead because no one wanted to tell them they were wrong." She has a lot to teach any of us. A fighter on and off the runway, in and out of the cockpit, Phillips has navigated many obstacles, including raising a special needs child and dealing with her own debilitating medical condition. With the medical profession, Phillips encounters confirmation bias, disregard, and incompetence from another set of professionals in charge of our lives. In emergency rooms and specialists' offices, she is called upon to speak up and fight for people's safety: this time, instead of a plane of passengers, for her daughter and herself.

The standard question Air Traffic Control asks a pilot when a plane is in jeopardy is "How many souls on board?" Phillips powerful book suggests that the cargo is human lives, but it's also human dignity. How we fly an airplane or navigate about this world is in no small part about how we treat—and how we should not treat— the colleagues and strangers around us.

Alexandria Peary
New Hampshire Poet Laureate, 2019-2024

The Making of a Flight Instructor

I was a twenty-two-year-old flight instructor the first time a student pilot surprised me in a big way. She was a new student in the glider with a cavalier approach to her flight training that belied a tendency to make bold and impulsive movements with the control stick. One of the early lessons involved learning about aerodynamics so I asked her to fly at a slower speed than normal. To slow down, she needed to raise the nose by applying some back pressure on the stick. Most student pilots cautiously raise the nose a little bit at a time and see what happens. My student yanked the stick all the way back into a vertical climb like she was trying to do a hammerhead. At the same time, she pushed down hard on the left rudder pedal with her foot, most likely to get more leverage on the stick. The combination of these two moves set us up perfectly to enter a spin. As the left wing dropped and the right wing slowly rose, we started corkscrewing in what seemed like slow motion toward the ground. All I could think about was that this glider was not approved for doing intentional spins, not because it couldn't get into one, but because it might not come out of one.

It had the aura of an out of body experience as I watched an apple orchard directly below us grow bigger through the glass canopy. My student, true to form, seemed not at all concerned. I put the stick and rudder pedals into the position recommended for "inadvertent" spin recovery and waited. Neat rows of apple trees became a few green canopies of trees, and then one tree's green leaves with red apples interspersed throughout. The tight circle we were making slowed until it eventually stopped, leaving us diving at the clearly visible apples on one tree, while quickly picking up speed. As I firmly pulled back on the stick so that only sky filled the canopy, I glanced to my left to assess my student's reaction. She looked bored.

This is one of the flight lessons I used from my personal experience to train pilots who were becoming flight instructors. Flight instructing is one of the few things you can do to earn the flying time necessary to move on to becoming an airline or corporate pilot outside of the military. Most pilots with only civilian flight experience become flight instructors soon after they earn their commercial pilot's certificate. It's unnatural in a way because it means that many of the instructors who are training new pilots are the least experienced commercial pilots. It's not the way it's done in many other parts of the world, but it's still the way we do it here in the United States. That is why I would share this story when teaching new instructors because it is an example of how a flight instructor must always be diligent when teaching others. This is especially true for those rare but scariest of all student pilots that make big moves as if you, the instructor, can get them out of anything. Thankfully most student pilots are more cautious than this student was, but it's safest to assume that they are all out to kill you—even if unintentionally.

When I first became a flight instructor at the age of twenty, I was often asked if I actually "flew in the airplane with students." I thought it was an odd question, but I guess the image of me teaching someone else how to fly was hard to imagine. They also might have thought that I taught things that pilots needed to know, like weather or navigation, from the safety of a classroom while someone else who looked like Charles Lindbergh got to teach the stuff that happens thousands of feet in the air. I also could pass for a thirteen-year-old girl, in my pigtails and T-shirts with funny sayings on them, which was far from looking like Tom Cruise in a flight suit.

What no one ever asked me was what I had to do to become a flight instructor. I could have told them how becoming a flight instructor was harder than flying in circles while trying to lower the landing gear with a contraption that looked like the old pull starters on my father's lawnmower—something I had to do once on a checkride. Becoming a flight instructor was difficult because flying the airplane was one thing, but explaining how to do it while demonstrating it was quite another.

I found flight instructing awkward at first. The airplanes I was flying had no intercom so everything I needed to convey had to be done at a high enough volume to be heard over the engine noise. I was not used to talking loudly because my mother suffered from debilitating migraine headaches after she fell ice skating and fractured her skull when I was ten. I dared not raise my voice above a whisper after I was told that my mother would end up in a psychiatric hospital if I was too loud. It's not surprising when my instructor first told me to loudly yell "clear" out the window before I started the airplane to warn anyone who might be near the propeller, I struggled to do it. And when I had to yell directions at him during instructor training to be heard over the noise of the engine, it felt doubly wrong.

After spending the summer break before my junior year of college teaching my instructor how to fly when he already knew how to do it better than me, I finally passed my checkride for my flight instructor certificate. I already had two students waiting to take lessons with me. One of those students was the fifteen-year-old son of a pilot and airplane owner who kept his airplane parked at the airport. He asked me to teach his son because he thought I could relate to him given that I had started taking lessons at a young age. Although I was only five years older than his son, it was clear from the start that he was immature for his age. I recognized the enormity of the responsibility I had taken on by the second lesson. I caught him fussing with his hair in the little mirror on the instrument panel when we were barely off the ground. Although I was never certain why that mirror was there, I was pretty sure it was not for this purpose.

Maybe the fact that his father had owned an airplane for much of his life made him take flying for granted, even though I found his father to be very down-to-earth and appreciative of his older model Cessna-172. Every lesson I found myself repeating the same things since this young man could not seem to recall anything we had done on the previous lesson. He also had clearly not cracked open a book because he couldn't answer any of my questions for him on the material I had assigned him to study. Soon I decided that I had to tell his father that he was wasting his money on flying lessons for his son at this time, and his father agreed with me. The lessons stopped until one day I ran into his father who told me that his son planned on going to a flight school in Florida after his high school graduation to train for all his pilot certificates at one time. I thought this might work out since he would have time to focus entirely on flying and would be three years older, and hopefully wiser, by then.

By the time this young man had returned from Florida with his commercial pilot certificate and his flight instructor certificate I had moved away, and his father had sold his airplane. My own father, who I had taught how to fly, hung out at the airport on weekends and had bought his own older model Cessna, and he called me one night to tell me that this young man and three of his friends from high school had died after they rented an airplane and were seen doing spins. My father had seen the foursome before they climbed into the airplane and had commented on how rambunctious and loud they had been. He felt like at least some of the guys had been drinking and someone had even intervened to try to stop them from going flying that Sunday afternoon. They were unsuccessful in preventing them from taking off even as they taxied in a haphazard fashion down the one taxiway that was visible from the window of the airport lounge.

When darkness set in and the airplane had not returned, reports started coming in from near the airport that the airplane had been seen doing multiple spins in a row. The last spin continued all the way to the ground. There were no survivors. This airplane was not approved for doing intentional spins when there were passengers or cargo in the back. This newly certified flight instructor must have known this because he had to demonstrate he could teach the aerodynamics behind spins for his instructor checkride. It was difficult to accept the preventable deaths of these four eighteen-year-olds, and to realize that this teenager still didn't respect the serious task of flying an airplane. I could only imagine the pain his father must have felt.

Nearly two decades later I found myself teaching young pilots to become flight instructors. In this role I got to fly like a student would, making many of the mistakes common to student pilots. One of the first aspiring flight instructors that I worked with seemed oblivious to the many "mistakes" I was making. He didn't say anything when I drifted off course, or when I seemingly ignored his instructions to fly at a particular altitude. After about twenty minutes of meandering around the sky, I asked him why he was letting all my mistakes go unchecked. I thought that perhaps now that he had to "pretend" that he was my instructor he felt awkward about pointing out my errors. I was a little deflated when he said, with zero sarcasm in his voice, "I wasn't sure if you were making mistakes on purpose or not and I didn't want to embarrass you in case *that was the best you could do.*" Wow.

I secretly thought that I was adept at playing the part of a student pilot, probably because I channeled how I acted as a fourteen-year-old taking flying lessons. I also think that some of the struggles I faced learning how to fly, whether because of my age, lack of life experience, or lack of hand-eye coordination, eventually paid off. I had learned more strategies for understanding what makes an airplane fly, or why carburetors develop ice when it's sixty degrees outside, because those concepts didn't come easily to me. Perhaps the biggest thing I had going for me as an instructor was a lack of swagger that put novice students at ease, and I tried to impress upon my fledgling instructors that it was often worthwhile to recall how they had felt early on in their flight training.

One thing I reminded aspiring instructors early in their training was to emphasize to their students the importance of being alert on the airport ramp. The ramp, where airplanes park and taxi, is full of potential threats. It has many of the same hazards as the flight deck of an aircraft carrier. Fuel or oil leaks on the pavement can make it as slippery as black ice. Ropes for tying down airplanes and chocks for keeping airplanes from moving can make the ramp seem like an obstacle course. At any moment a propeller can spin to life and jet engines can suck in anything that gets too close. I reminded new instructors that anyone, even experienced pilots, can become complacent and miss things in their surroundings that should have been obvious.

I often illustrated this point by sharing the story of a Cessna-172 that had been flown by four different pilots in a row before a student pilot noticed a softball-sized hole underneath the horizontal stabilizer. It turned out that an instructor and their student had hit a tree branch while trying to land on a small runway. Not wanting to get into trouble, they didn't report the mishap and the damage they had done to the airplane. Even more shocking, two of the pilots who flew the airplane afterward without noticing the hole were flight instructors—not new students. Since control cables run through that section of the tail, there could have been damage to the surfaces that allow the pilot to raise and lower the nose.

    I often wondered, like I imagine all teachers do, if anything I was saying was having any impact. This included the flight instructors that I supervised in our flight training program. After all, since I was teaching at a college, nearly all the instructors I was overseeing were twenty-one or twenty-two-year-old males who are not known for being the most risk averse demographic. I sometimes felt like they were humoring me, nodding appropriately to what I was saying, without hearing me. I had tried several times to caution the instructors that they should watch their students as they did their preflight inspections. This is when a pilot (or student pilot) does some checks in the cockpit like turning on lights and checking the fuel gauges, and then closely looks at the entire exterior of the airplane to make sure it is airworthy. Some of the instructors would wait inside while their students did the preflight and then hop in the airplane without ever checking to see if their students had missed something. I was guilty of this too at times, but I had enough experience, and had been through enough scary situations, that I knew better than to assume the airplane was ready to fly just because a student said it was. I had seen flat tires, bird nests in the front of the engine or in the tail section (not sure how they got in there), and big dents in a wing that went unnoticed by student pilots who assured me that the airplane was ready to fly. This can happen for a lot of reasons, but it's particularly difficult for new students to notice problems because they have not been around airplanes long enough to have seen all the issues that can occur. Often, everything is fine, so they don't see something that is unexpected and out of the norm.

Then one day an opportunity presented itself to demonstrate this problem to a bunch of new instructors. They were sipping their first coffee of the day in the dispatch area where students received the keys to their airplanes, and where there were several large windows where you could observe the ramp. None of them were paying much attention to what was going on as their students did their preflight inspections. I saw that one of our gliders was parked on the ramp with its right wing removed for repair. The person handing out the keys that morning was a longtime colleague with a great sense of humor, and he agreed with me that it would be "educational" to give a student the keys to this glider and ask him to do his preflight inspection. Then we could watch unnoticed from the office window to see how long it would take him to realize the glider was missing an entire wing.

I knew the preflight checklist for the glider began in the cockpit and moved to the tail before proceeding to the right wing. It was the perfect setup to see if he was paying attention or merely going through the motions of checking the condition of the glider. I speculated that he would walk across the ramp to the glider, with the missing wing clearly visible the whole time, and then do all the checks in the cockpit and inspect the left side all the way to the tail before he would get to the right side and finally notice the missing wing. There was some disagreement among the instructors as to whether this would happen, and I believe a wager may have been involved—all in the service of aviation safety.

Sure enough, the student did exactly as I had predicted as we all watched. He looked closely at the entire left side of the glider and the tail before walking around to the missing right wing. He paused when he got to the missing wing, looking startled and a bit confused, and then he did what we all would likely do—he sheepishly looked up at the window to see if anyone was watching. We all waved and smiled at him, and being someone who had his own sense of humor, he took a bow as if he was in on the gag the whole time. I had made my point.

Another strategy I used while teaching flight instructors was to "sabotage" the airplane to see if they caught the potential hazards. This involved doing things that could be unsafe if they were not noticed and corrected. Much like needing to keep a tally of where I put all the eggs for an Easter egg hunt so that none were left behind to ferment under a pillow, this practice required a high level of diligence on my part. It was also my policy to only make mistakes that students had made in the past with me. I left baggage doors unlatched, put the flaps all the way down for takeoff, set the heading indicator to the wrong heading, and closed the door on my seat belt so it would bang loudly after takeoff if left undiscovered. Once we got off the ground, I did what one of my favorite students did when he first started flying with me—I made all my turns in the opposite direction of where I should have been going.

Another one of my favorite things to do was to slowly drift off course during a lesson where they were supposed to be teaching me about navigation. By doing it in small increments I hoped they would realize that even being just a few miles off course can lead to a situation where they wander into a part of the sky where they shouldn't be. It's much easier to stay on course when you are navigating yourself, but it can be too easy to let a student drift off and not notice they are in restricted airspace. This can lead to a violation (like a traffic ticket) from the FAA, and that can prevent someone from getting a job as a pilot, or keeping the job they already have. In some cases, it can even lead to jet fighters coming up alongside you and forcing you to land or risk getting shot down. It doesn't matter if the mistake is made by a student instead of the instructor because ultimately the instructor is the one who is responsible for the safety of the flight. The student is never at fault if an instructor is on board, and that is how it should be. Two flight instructors I worked with got in trouble for veering off course during two different flight lessons and flying too close to the airspace around the White House and around the summer home of the Bush family in Kennebunkport, Maine. Fortunately, these incidents both happened before September 11, 2001, when everyone got less alarmed about such things.

Just like I had to caution aspiring instructors about the lackadaisical student who seemed fearless, I also taught instructors about what to do if a student was frozen in fear on the flight controls. This is not common because students who are scared are more likely to let go of the flight controls, but it happened to me, and I was glad I was prepared for it. I was flying with a short, ruggedly built guy with a serious demeanor who I had just met. His physique reminded me of my fifth-grade teacher and softball coach, Mr. Robtoy, who had previously trained for the Olympic wrestling team. Quiet and compact, this guy was already tense, and he didn't seem pleased that I was filling in for his regular instructor on a frigid winter Saturday. All my other lessons that day had been canceled because of snow showers, but finally there was a break in the clouds. I was aware that snow showers can move in quickly, but the visibility was good, so we could see any approaching bands of intense showers known as snow squalls.

As it turned out, we were flying for about a half-hour when I saw the telltale sheets of white indicating that snow was approaching from the west. We headed back to the airport with my student flying to keep him distracted from the weather behind him. Tiny snow pellets began bouncing off the windshield as we lined up for our final turn toward the runway. We were about six-hundred feet above the ground and had the runway clearly in sight. I was talking him through the approach. He was silent the whole time, so I couldn't get a good read on how he was feeling. Although this was the first time he had seen snow pellets or any form of precipitation from the cockpit of an airplane, I reassured him there was no reason for concern.

He appeared mesmerized by how the pellets hitting the windshield can give you a sense of speed, making you feel like you are launching into space. I admit that it's an intoxicating experience the first time you see it. What I failed to recognize was what I thought was fascination with this new sight was better described as terror. Without warning he began pushing the nose toward the ground. He had both of his hands on the yoke with his fingers in a tight grip and his elbows locked. I calmly but emphatically told him to pull the nose back up while I reached for the flight controls. When he continued to push forward, causing us to momentarily rise out of our seats, I yelled, "I've got the airplane." Normally a student would immediately let go of the flight controls, but he did not. He continued to push us toward the ground, and I yelled again for him to let go. He wouldn't budge, and I was unable to counteract the force he was applying to the yoke.

As the frozen ground below filled the windshield, I knew the time for talking him through it was gone. When I was in training to be a flight instructor, I had been taught a strategy for getting the flight controls back from a terrified student. At the time I couldn't imagine myself ever doing it, but when faced with imminent impact with the ground, I got over any qualms I had. I took my left hand off the controls and backhanded him hard across the nose. This had the desired effect as he was startled enough to let go of the yoke. He spent the remaining minutes of the flight silent with his head down, nursing a bleeding nose. Once we got on the ground, he fled out the door, not giving me time to even fill out his logbook. It left me wondering if I had just uncovered a reason why he shouldn't continue flying, or if I had just inadvertently crushed his lifelong dream.

Perhaps that was the trickiest part of being a flight instructor, knowing when it's best to let a student walk away from something they are not well suited for, or when you need to build up someone's confidence so that they can achieve their dream of flying. I might not have been able to teach them how to make that call without some experience, but I at least wanted to share all the experiences I had so that instructors I worked with would fly another day.

Twins

My fascination with flying started early. I was in the second grade when my teacher, Mrs. Wilkinson, asked us to write a few sentences about what kind of animal we would be if we could choose just one. Without hesitation I printed *I want to be a bird so I can fly*. Seven years later, at the age of fourteen, I took my first flying lesson.

I didn't know then that the first female pilot for a major U.S. airline had been hired just one year earlier. I'm not sure it would have deterred me from becoming a commercial pilot even if I knew how few women flew airplanes for a living. Even at a young age, I never felt like my pursuits were limited by my gender. I can trace the source of that understanding back to Christmas morning in 1968, when my identical twin sister, Sherry, and I were five years old. That Christmas my mother bought us toy toolkits so we could help our father build a bookcase in the garage. Inside the shiny white and red metal boxes were some nails, a small hammer, a miniature saw, and a few other items of interest to an aspiring carpenter. Our mother grew agitated as she stared at the toolboxes. On the front lid was a picture of a young boy staring lovingly at his father, with a caption that read, "For a boy to help his dad."

"Don't pay attention to that," my mother said, clearly exasperated, in contrast to her usual festive mood on Christmas morning. "Girls can use hammers too," she said with a defiant tone in her voice that surprised me.

My mother was an unlikely feminist. She was so gender

conforming in her parenting style that she only sewed dresses and skirts for Sherry and me. As we got older, she made us wear pink plastic curlers in our hair while we slept to achieve the desired feminine waves and curls. These were not the flexible styling tools that exist today but rigid inflictors of pain that jabbed when you rolled onto your back. Despite her insistence on femininity in her daughters, my mother was disgusted that this toy was targeted at boys. She knew how much Sherry and I liked to hang out with our father in the garage as he attempted various woodworking projects. She was worried that we might think there was something wrong with that.

My mother had good reason to be concerned. There was already ample evidence that I was baffled about issues related to gender. In the fall prior to that Christmas, my confusion became apparent when Sherry and I were asked to appear in a fashion show for a children's boutique in town. I loved that store on Main Street packed full of brightly colored clothes for girls and boys. There were the ever-popular sailor suits for boys, and racks of lace-trimmed dresses for girls. Sherry and I were asked to model for the show even though our mother never bought any clothes there. She made it clear that she could make us dresses on her Singer for a fraction of the price whenever I coveted something from the window display. I suspect that the spectacle of identical twins outweighed the fact that my mother was not a shopper there.

My initial excitement over the fashion show quickly disappeared when it was decided that I would model a bright orange pantsuit with a matching belt. I had never worn a belt before (or pants, for that matter), and I was convinced that wearing these items of clothing would make everyone think that I was a boy. My sister, who always seemed to get the better end of the deal, got to wear an above-the-knee dress that was a beautiful shade of blue on the bottom with a contrasting yellow plaid on top. Blue was my favorite color, and I loved plaid. Sherry looked chic and feminine while my bright orange blazer and coordinating pants were gaudy and clearly made for a boy (preferably a colorblind one).

We were supposed to walk out together like some bizarre boy/girl pair. Although we had been raised to be obedient and to never "talk back" to our mother, for the first time in my short life I put the possible punishments aside and steadfastly refused to go on stage. This led Sherry to have her own meltdown because there was no way she was going out on that stage alone, but she was excited to be able to twirl elegantly in front of the crowd in her dress. I was finally convinced to go on for her sake. I was still pouting as they pulled open the curtain, which might have worked for a supermodel, but wasn't a great look for a children's fashion show. Ironically, I would later learn that my desire to fly like a bird would mean that I would not only have to wear pants, but also a blazer, and a men's black tie—the traditional uniform of an airline pilot.

In many ways the conspicuousness of being an identical twin helped prepare me for entering a profession where I would stand out simply because of my gender. Being an identical twin in our town of less than six-thousand people in the sixties was a conspicuous event. Much like some popular reality T.V. shows today, my childhood was often on display. The town newspaper, *The Puddledock Press,* lacking much actual news, instead carried stories and photos of social events like our tenth birthday party—including a list of guests and family members in attendance.

Being an identical twin brought both joy and frustration. My earliest memory of Sherry is of her twisting a vacuum cleaner hose around my neck. Fortunately for me, our father intervened. I don't recall what sparked Sherry's desire to strangle me, but I am sure it had to do with one of my many offenses in her mind, the biggest of which was looking and talking just like her. The feeling was mutual.

Not long after the botched attempt at strangulation, Sherry got in trouble for running in the house. Our two-bedroom New Englander built around 1910 had five small rooms on two floors and its design was the opposite of today's open floor plans. Our mother had strict rules about not running in the house. Ironically, the punishment for running in the house or other infractions was a spanking with a wooden paddle she saved from one of those bouncing paddle ball games. On the day in question, I saw her getting out the paddle, secretly relishing the fact she was headed for Sherry this time—only she wasn't. The sting of the paddle was not nearly as hurtful as the fact that she got us mixed up. As time went on and our mother's patience dwindled, she would spank both of us whenever we fought. The message was clear—it didn't matter who started the fight.

Punishing us both equally was consistent with my mother's belief that the best way to raise identical twins was to ensure we were treated exactly alike. Each Christmas our mother bought us the same gifts regardless of what we had asked for that year. Each gift was wrapped with identical wrapping paper, then each pair of presents was assigned a number instead of a name. We spent Christmas morning opening the packages in unison like some kind of holiday synchronized swimming event. Before long we started opening gifts out of order to deliberately spoil the suspense. We just wanted recognition that we were not the same, that Sherry's favorite color was purple and mine was blue, that Sherry wanted a bracelet, and I coveted some leather boots.

At school, every one of my academic achievements was evaluated not on its own merits, but on how it compared to Sherry and vice versa. Although our father tried harder to treat us as individuals, he also fumbled at times. I remember telling him that I had been named valedictorian of our graduating class. His first words were, "How did your sister do?" (For the record, she was third). Our SAT scores were compared not to the average scores for colleges we might want to attend, but to each other's scores. Even our IQ scores, which were within 5 points of each other, were revealed to us as if that difference was somehow significant.

My home life was further complicated by the fact that my mother was the most anxious person I have ever known, even if at the time I didn't know the word to describe her behavior. The list of things my mother feared was long and nonsensical, and the way she dealt with her fears was to try to control everything around her. Trash was wrapped up neatly in brown paper bags, then stapled shut with four precise corners so that it looked like a gift bag rather than the garbage that it was. It wasn't until my first sleepover that I realized other mothers didn't line up seven bars of soap, each in its own white dish, to be used for each day of the week. Her fear of thunderstorms was so great that she climbed into bed with the covers over her head at the first rumble of thunder. She wouldn't let us open any windows, even on the hottest of days, because of her fear of insects and spiders. She was so anxious about driving that she would pull into the breakdown lane on the right side of the road to build up the courage to make a left turn.

In all fairness to our parents, they were stunned at our birth. Apparently, the doctor only detected one heartbeat, and without ultrasound, our twin birth was a surprise. Part of the inclination to treat identical twins as one person might also have to do with the definition of the word "identical." If you google the definition, you get the following: similar in every detail; exactly alike. Synonyms include words like indistinguishable and interchangeable. Dr. Benjamin Spock described a twin birth as an "anomaly" and a "curiosity." Parenting books from the fifties and still widely in use included information on twins under a section entitled "special problems." No wonder our parents were mystified about how to raise us.

To Sherry and me, our differences were obvious. When we looked in the mirror, we didn't see a carbon copy of ourselves. (Although I admit to once attending an aviation conference with Sherry and thinking that she was walking toward me when it was my reflection in a mirror). The constant comparisons made us want to distinguish ourselves in whatever small ways that we could. Once our mother finally let us choose our own clothes, Sherry always wore a belt and tucked in her shirts, while I didn't even own a belt. (Perhaps my memories of the fashion show and that belted orange jumpsuit had something to do with it). We were also set up to compete for everything. My father frequently recalls how he had to break up a fight between us over who got the best pile of snow in our backyard for making a fort on the day after a blizzard. By the time Sherry and I reached the age of fourteen, we craved a chance to break free of each other and lead independent lives.

Our father was the one who first got us interested in aviation. While in the Marine Corps, he was responsible for preparing and loading weapons onto airplanes during the Korean War. He dreamed of becoming a pilot one day even though he was too nearsighted to fly in the military. His desire to fly never wavered even as any money he might have spent on flying lessons was used to buy two of everything for his twin daughters.

So, in some ways it was not surprising that on a hot summer day after Sherry and I had played so many games of badminton, catch, and ping pong we could no longer stand the sight of each other, Dad drove us to the airport. It was July 27, 1977, and Skyhaven Airport in Rochester, New Hampshire had a single three-thousand-foot runway and a couple of two-seat training airplanes you could rent for a short lesson with an instructor. The importance of that first flight was so clear to me then that I still have the receipt showing that my father paid ten dollars in cash for a flight in a Cessna-150 with the tail number of N714CG. By the time I landed, with the instructor letting me do much of the flying from the left seat, I was certain that becoming a commercial pilot was my destiny. I knew I had my father's support when I saw him take some cash he had hidden in his sock drawer to buy me my first logbook and flight manual. In return I promised him that I would give him free flying lessons when I became a flight instructor.

Although Sherry soon started taking flying lessons too, for her flying was something she would do for fun, but not as a profession. She had long aspired to work in finance and accounting and earn enough money to buy her own airplane. I didn't care how much money I made so long as I was getting paid to fly.

When I started flying by myself to other airports, I realized it was the first time in my life I was doing something without Sherry by my side. Although we both soloed for the first time on the same day at the age of sixteen and got our private pilot certificates on our seventeenth birthday, once I began pursuing flying professionally, I was truly on my own. The people I met on the ground and the air traffic controllers I talked to in the air had no idea that I was an identical twin. It was disorienting at first after so many years of being compared to my sister, but I soon realized how freeing it was to fly to new places by myself and to be treated as an individual instead of one-half of a pair. That feeling didn't last long.

One day I flew to an airport that Sherry had flown into the day before in the same airplane. I had not given any thought to how similar our voices were on the radio and how that might be perceived. I was feeling proud of my navigation skills in finding this airport that was more than one-hundred miles away from Skyhaven. It was the longest flight I had ever done. After a smooth landing, I transmitted to Ground Control, "Cessna niner-two uniform requests progressive taxi instructions to the ramp." This was a way of letting the controller know that I was unfamiliar with this airport and its many taxiways and was requesting step by step instructions. A few seconds later I was reminded that I couldn't escape being a twin so easily when I heard the reply from the male controller: "Jeez lady, you were just here yesterday. Can't you remember how to get there?"

Checkrides

Professional pilots get tested a lot. Not only do they have to take written tests to become a private pilot, commercial pilot, or to get their instrument rating so they can fly in bad weather, but they must also take practical tests, typically referred to as checkrides. On each checkride a pilot must demonstrate they can perform a long list of flying skills. Checkrides are administered largely by a group of experienced aviators called designated pilot examiners. I was likely one of the youngest designated pilot examiners in the country (and undoubtedly the youngest female examiner) when I was selected by the FAA at the age of twenty-four. Most of my peers were men in their sixties and seventies. I suspect that turnover in the field of pilot examiners is about the same as it is for Supreme Court justices—and for similar reasons.

Training for being a designated pilot examiner consists of several days of indoctrination at the FAA headquarters in Oklahoma City. I remember being excited on my flight out of Boston because the skies were clear all the way to our cruising altitude. This allowed me to clearly make out landmarks like the muddy Mississippi River. I had never been west of it before. Once we landed in Oklahoma City and I was on my way to my hotel, I felt eerily out of place when I saw that many of the highway billboards were welcoming newcomers to the area's many strip clubs. The signs only multiplied as we got closer to my hotel, making me wonder if this was part of a plan by the FAA to save money on our accommodations.

I had never traveled so far from home by myself before.

Everything from the cowboy hats to the oil rigs that dotted the horizon were new to me. Since none of the nearby eating establishments looked like places where I wanted to venture out to by myself in the dark, and there was no room service at the hotel, I ate what I could find out of the vending machines on that first night. I already was suffering from a serious case of imposter syndrome and the fact that I was called "little lady" several times that first evening didn't help. I went to bed early and tried to lull myself to sleep with music from the clock radio, but all I could find was country music and people talking loudly about Jesus.

The next morning, I wasn't feeling any less out of place, and like many people who are nervous I spent a considerable amount of time pondering what I should wear. It was one of those times when I envied the fact that men can just grab a tie and be done with it. I decided to go with a black pair of feminine trousers and a white button-down blouse for my first day. I didn't have many options anyway because on my salary as an instructor I barely made enough money to pay rent on my small apartment. Buying professional attire was also a bit of a waste given that I was likely to get fuel, hydraulic fluid, or oil on my pants by lunchtime.

As I walked into the typical conference room with long tables arranged in a rectangle, there were some catering staff serving coffee and arranging bagels and muffins as part of a small buffet. The wait staff were all women wearing black trousers and white blouses very similar to mine. I was one of the first to arrive, and so I stood awkwardly waiting as men, dressed in everything from three-piece suits to blue jeans and nearly all in their sixties and seventies, began to arrive. I envied how they seemed so comfortable and confident, sharing flying tales and sizing each other up. I was never good at casual banter, especially in a room full of older men, and I kept looking at my watch to see if it was time to take our seats. I am also not a coffee drinker, and it seemed like I was the only one without a coffee cup in my hand—which likely contributed to what happened next.

As I fidgeted in the corner, one of the men casually walked up to me and asked if I could refill his coffee cup. My first thought was *What do I look like, one of the wait staff* and quickly realized that indeed I did. It occurred to me that I could just introduce myself, but I felt bad for this guy who had made an understandable mistake given my unfortunate choice of attire. I was more concerned about embarrassing him than clarifying what my role was there, and so I said, "Certainly," and took his cup over to refill it. As I was doing this, another man approached me and asked for some water, and I directed him to the bottles that were at the far end of the table. If he also expected me to fetch it for him, he said nothing, for which I was grateful. It never occurred to me that these guys might be even more embarrassed in a few minutes when we all sat down and introduced ourselves.

Maybe I should have been indignant that no one considered that I might be a pilot too, but being confrontational was never my way. I once listened to two nicely dressed, clean cut young men talk about the *Book of Mormon* for two hours because I thought it was rude to ask them to leave. I've always been a quiet person, an introvert, who likes to think things over before offering my opinion. Given that I already felt out of place, I didn't want to be more conspicuous by correcting these two men. Up until this point in my career, no one had ever assumed I was a pilot—not even when they saw me climb out of the left seat of the cockpit. Sometimes a person working on the airport ramp would look for the pilot when I showed up by myself in an airplane, as if maybe he was asleep in the back seat.

Once examiner training began, I immediately felt more

comfortable, buoyed by my supportive colleagues—especially the two who originally thought I was a waitress. They were impressed by my flying credentials at such a young age, and several of them with rental cars offered to take me to dinner each night and brought me back and forth to training each day so that I didn't need to take a cab. There was one other female pilot there who flew gliders exclusively and was in her late fifties, and one male pilot who was close to me in age. Many of my colleagues were retired airline pilots or owners of flight schools. Several told me that they had never flown with a female pilot, and some who had were eager to share how competent and professional their female colleagues were. A few of the pilots quietly admitted that flying with female co-pilots was a refreshing break from the competitiveness and one upmanship that often prevailed in the cockpit when they flew with a male co-pilot.

One of the odd things we practiced during examiner training was how to be expressionless when quizzing someone on a checkride. The idea was to not give away any hints as to whether the applicant was right or wrong when being asked to explain such things as the mechanics of the landing gear system in their airplane, or what to do if they lost radio communications with air traffic control while flying in the clouds. I thought the FAA might have taken this testing technique too far, especially when they got out several full-size mirrors and made each of us practice administering an oral test while looking as animated as someone who had too much Botox.

Despite how I felt about this exercise, I immediately saw an opportunity to make an impression by showing how robotic I could be. I practiced at night in my hotel room since I had plenty of time on my hands given the local entertainment venues. I was rewarded by the stunned appreciation of my colleagues and trainers the next day when it was my turn to demonstrate my newfound skills. I worked out a way to combine a small frown with a questioning look to give the impression that whatever answer the pilot gave me was wrong. Being deadpan was one thing, but perfecting how to make even the cockiest pilot question themselves was even better in the minds of the folks at the FAA. I finally felt like I belonged here.

It was a relief when examiner training was complete, and I could set out to become the type of examiner that I wanted to be. One of the things that influenced me the most was my recent experience taking checkrides myself. While most of my colleagues at examiner training had not taken a checkride for many years, I had just completed two checkrides: one so that I could instruct pilots in airplanes with two engines, and the other for my airline transport certificate. Those experiences made me keenly aware of how an examiner with an attitude could make a checkride more hellish than it needs to be.

Just a few months before I went to Oklahoma, I had to find someone who could do the two checkrides I needed in a Cessna T303 Crusader. This airplane, designed as a training aircraft but with added features like two turbocharged engines, and seating for five passengers in a spacious cabin, was not a common airplane to use for a checkride. Despite being a joy to fly, the untimeliness of its introduction to the aviation market meant that only two-hundred ninety-seven Crusaders were ever built. This meant that there were few pilot examiners who had ever flown one, and even fewer who had taken the time to get certified to administer checkrides in it.

I was eventually able to find an examiner in Massachusetts who could do the checkrides I needed, but no one could tell me anything about him. Just like a lawyer may prefer to argue their cases before certain judges that they know either personally or by reputation, pilots like to know something about the person who is going to be testing them. The informal word of mouth that goes around about different examiners and their likes and dislikes can help boost a pilot's confidence before a checkride. I wasn't going to have this insider knowledge going for me. He was also not going to know anything about me, which unfortunately usually meant that he would form his first impressions based on his experiences with any other female pilots he might have flown with—if any.

When I arrived for my checkride, the examiner was being interviewed by a local television station about the recent crash of a small airplane nearby. I could tell by his demeanor that the interview was not going well. He seemed perturbed about the questions the reporter was asking him, and I thought this could not be a good omen for me. I was right. He took his time ending the interview as if we didn't have an appointment. Then he took one look at me and, without so much as a single word of introduction, told me to draw a diagram of the fuel system of the Crusader while motioning to a nearby chalkboard.

It's not that expecting me to know the fuel system so thoroughly that I could draw it was unfair—it was not. The problem was that I have never been able to draw unless I was copying a picture someone else had drawn. I used to copy my favorite comic strips of Snoopy and the Red Baron, even winning a blue ribbon when I was nine after recreating a drawing of Snoopy and Linus in the pumpkin patch, but when I had to draw something that supposedly was in my head, it was like there was a short circuit between my brain and my hand.

I figured I had nothing to lose, so I told the examiner, who was now looking at me like I shouldn't be allowed to fly a kite, that I couldn't draw the fuel system. In retrospect I think that he was already forming an unfavorable impression about me because

I had to bring another instructor along for the flight. It was an insurance requirement until I passed the checkride that I needed to fly the Crusader with an instructor, but to the examiner it probably looked like no one trusted me to fly the airplane by myself. I told the examiner that I knew every detail about the fuel system in the Crusader, but that I much preferred to describe it to him than draw it. He looked dubious but he listened intently while I described the location and purpose of every part of the fuel system. Fortunately, he was satisfied with my explanation in the end, while still not comprehending why I couldn't draw something that I could describe in such detail. I told him that I didn't understand it either, which seemed to soften him a bit.

Although I passed the oral test, I still had to prove to him that I could fly. The FAA publishes a list of items that a person taking a checkride is required to demonstrate to the examiner. It is not meant to be suggestive or a guide; it is meant to be a comprehensive list of specific maneuvers that must be performed on every test. It is intended to standardize checkrides for everyone, but this examiner had a different agenda for me. Since this checkride was for the purpose of certifying me to be an instructor on multi-engine airplanes, it was supposed to focus on my ability to teach in this airplane. He had other ideas.

He never asked me to teach him anything, but instead made me fly this airplane with every conceivable combination of mechanical and equipment failures. He simulated an engine failure by pulling back the power on one of the engines, which was expected, but then he also covered up nearly all the flight instruments too. This violated one of the rules regarding checkrides. As a pilot examiner, you are only allowed to simulate abnormal situations that could realistically occur together. It was extremely unlikely for an engine to fail at the same time as nearly all the flight instruments. Not only does the loss of an engine not affect the flight instruments, but the instruments are powered by different sources too, so they won't fail all at once. For instance, some of them are electrically powered while others rely on pumps driven by the engine. If a pilot found themselves in the predicament that he put me in, then they are having a freakishly bad day. Clearly, he intended to give me a freakishly bad time.

Just when I thought it couldn't get any worse, he made me do a nondirectional beacon (NDB) approach. This is an instrument approach where you fly an established procedure using only the flight instruments by navigating off the radio signal from a transmitter on the ground. The NDB approach is arguably the most difficult kind of approach to do because it requires the pilot to calculate and fly a precise heading to stay on course to a runway. This is nearly impossible to do without the heading indicator that he had covered up. No pilot in their right mind would ever choose to fly an NDB approach without a heading indicator and with one of their engines out. In the end I managed to handle everything that he could come up with and I passed the two and a half-hour checkride, but I was grinding my teeth the whole time because I was so mad.

A few months later I had to return for a second checkride for my airline transport certificate. This is supposed to be the toughest of all the checkrides because it's the gateway to flying for an airline, the PhD of flight certificates. After my previous checkride with this examiner, I worried what hellish scenario he would come up with for me this time. It turned out to be the easiest checkride I had ever taken. Apparently, he had run out of ideas, or maybe he was finally convinced that I knew what I was doing. This experience made me think carefully about what kind of pilot examiner I wanted to be. I wasn't going to treat being a pilot examiner as some kind of power trip, but as an opportunity to give everyone a fair checkride.

After completing examiner training, I had to do one more thing before I could start giving checkrides. I had to do a checkride while a representative from the FAA rode in the back and observed. The most challenging part of this was that I needed to find a pilot who was ready for a checkride and who was willing to do this. It's a given that no one likes to fly with someone from the FAA watching their pilot examiner's every move. They know the pilot examiner must be especially careful to not let anything slip by. It's an added source of stress during a checkride that no one wants to take on voluntarily and I had a hard time finding someone willing to do their checkride in this way. I also had to find someone who was ready to take their checkride in the Cessna Crusader so that I could be certified to do checkrides in that airplane. I finally decided to ask a student named Tim who I had flown with before and who seemed to me to be cool under pressure.

On the day that Tim and I were to fly to the airport where the local FAA office was located, there was a dry cold front approaching. This meant that although there would be clear skies, the wind was forecasted to increase rapidly as the front passed through the area. There was a weather advisory issued for gusts to forty knots later in the day, accompanied by moderate turbulence. Tim and I had waited for over a month to get on the FAA inspector's schedule, so we didn't want to reschedule despite the anticipated turbulence. Yet I also knew from personal experience that flying in the back of the Crusader was the worst place to be in turbulence. You always get bounced around more in the back (note to anyone who easily gets airsick—try to get a seat near the front of the airplane) and in the Crusader it was harder to see out the window from the back. Both factors, along with a lack of fresh air vents, could make even the hardiest of fliers wish they were back on solid ground. So, I was pleasantly surprised when the FAA representative said he was willing to fly in this weather.

Tim and I had a pleasant and relatively smooth flight following the coastline from Nashua, New Hampshire to Portland, Maine. We also knew that we were flying away from the front, and that on the way back we would be flying into the approaching cold front. Tim, who was a native of Bermuda and as mellow and unflappable as an ocean breeze, was visibly nervous. I tried to cheer him up by reminding him that our "passenger" would be testing me and not him. Still, I had never seen Tim sweat so much, and he even asked me to fly part of the way so that he could admire the scenery and calm his nerves.

By the time we landed in Portland, the wind had started to pick up and we were getting thrashed around by the turbulence. I could see whitecaps forming on the waves just offshore. The FAA inspector, clearly aware of the incoming front, quickly strapped himself into the seat behind me. He was an intimidating looking man in his seventies who said little but had a reputation for being fair. I suspect that he wanted to get this flight over with as much as we did before the winds picked up.

As I had Tim go through the maneuvers required for the test, the choppiness of the air was increasing to the point where we were constantly bouncing up and down. We tightened our seatbelts and shoulder harnesses as much as we could, and I tried to get through everything as quickly as possible while not rushing Tim. He was doing fine despite the conditions, right up to where he made a mistake while flying an instrument approach wearing foggles so that he could only see his flight instruments. Foggles are like a pair of goggles that are painted over so that the only thing a pilot can see are their flight instruments. (Think of goggles for simulating what it is like flying in fog when you can't see outside.) There was a little jog in the otherwise straight path to the runway where Tim needed to fly a few degrees in a new direction. Tim missed this little notation on the chart. It was an easy mistake to make, but one that could put us clearly off course to the runway. I suspected that the FAA inspector in the back was so focused on not barfing that he had not yet noticed Tim's mistake. The longer we flew in this direction the more obvious it would become that we were off course.

I needed to figure out a way to get Tim to notice his error without alerting the inspector. I knew that having an FAA inspector in the back observing your checkride is as relaxing as driving a car with a police car behind you. I already felt guilty for putting Tim through this and if he failed this checkride over this we would have to do this flight over again—and I would blame myself. I felt like what I imagine the parent of a child in the final round of the Scripps Spelling Bee must feel when a complicated word is announced. I suspect if the parent knows how to spell the word they will mentally try to communicate the letters to their son or daughter. I was trying to will Tim into rechecking his chart for the correct course in much the same way, but it wasn't working. I needed to do something surreptitiously to salvage this.

I knew from examiner training that we were allowed to distract the pilot being tested to see if they maintained their focus on flying the airplane. So, I started to ask Tim some questions. I could see him giving me the side eye as if to say *Really, you're going to do this now,* but I pressed on, hoping it would save him in the end. I started off asking him what altitude he was allowed to descend to in the hopes of obscuring my real intention. Then I asked him as casually as I could muster, "What is the final course to the runway?" Tim glanced down at his chart, and he immediately saw his error and adjusted his course. If the inspector noticed, he said nothing. I breathed a sigh of relief knowing that all we had left to do was to shut down one engine and restart it. That was relatively straightforward, but it was also the riskiest part of any checkride in a multi-engine airplane. When I announced my plan to have Tim shut down the engine, the FAA inspector shot back, "Uh, that's all right. Let's get on the ground." Apparently, he had seen enough. Tim had passed his checkride and was now a commercial pilot, but we still had to get home.

The winds were howling by now, over sixty knots at an altitude of just three-thousand feet and gusting to forty knots on the ground. We briefly contemplated taking a bus home and coming back for the airplane later, but in the end, we decided thirty minutes of thrashing around the skies was better than several hours on a bus. We climbed high enough to avoid the worst of the turbulence, but we knew the landing approach back at our home airport was going to be a rough ride—like riding one of those bucking broncos at a rodeo. Tim was so exhausted from having to take his checkride under these stressful conditions that he asked me to fly us back while he took a break—and I was happy to do it.

It was a heady feeling getting to issue pilot certificates and knowing that I was playing a role in a pilot's most important accomplishments. Like with many other times in my flying career when I started to feel a sense of pride, there was someone ready to keep me humble. One day soon after I became an examiner, a student pilot scheduled his private pilot checkride with me. I had never flown with him, and he seemed not at all intimidated by the fact that this was his first checkride. He was almost a little too cocky, so to challenge him I started asking him questions while he was getting himself into the traffic pattern to prepare for landing. There were a lot of other airplanes trying to land that day, and so I kept asking him if he saw each airplane as they announced their position over the radio—partly to make sure we kept our distance, and partly to see if he would let it interfere with his flying. After the third time I asked him if he saw one of the other airplanes ahead of us, trying to be as casual as I could, he said, "Can you shut up because I'm trying to fly an airplane here!" It was the best checkride I had ever done.

My First Day as a Professional Pilot

I was twenty years old and had my commercial pilot's license for less than twenty-four hours when I got my first job as a pilot. I was hired to fly to an airshow in Concord, New Hampshire, where I would take passengers up for rides. I had put all the money I made working multiple jobs toward paying for flying lessons. I had worked at the local airport washing airplanes and pumping fuel, I babysat four children at a time who never went to bed, and I shoveled all the neighbors' driveways back when snowfall in New Hampshire was as common as rain in Seattle. Now, six years after my first flying lesson, I would take up my first paying passengers.

I didn't look like most of the pilots I knew. Besides the fact that fewer than 4 percent of commercial pilots in 1983 were women, I also looked young for my age. I had no fancy uniform that identified me as a pilot. I was petite enough that I used a blue boat cushion to boost myself up high enough in the seat of the Cessna to see over the nose for landing. It occurred to me that some parents might balk at buying a ride for their kids when they saw I was their pilot.

On my checkride the day before for my commercial pilot's certificate, I had to fly two airplanes while someone from the FAA observed my every move. As part of my test, I had to calculate how various combinations of fuel, passengers, and baggage could be loaded into several different airplanes. Every airplane has a maximum weight limit, as well as restrictions on how the weight can be distributed in the airplane, known as weight and balance limitations. Too much weight in the back makes the airplane too tail heavy and too much in the front makes it too nose heavy. The entire checkride had taken most of the day, but now I could get paid to fly. I had been offered twenty-five dollars for the day for flying passengers at the airshow. I would have done it for free.

The airplane I was flying was one of the most popular airplanes ever built. It was a Cessna Skyhawk, also known as a Cessna-172, and it had two seats in the back and two in the front for a total of three passengers and a pilot. In this airplane, I knew that with the fuel tanks nearly full of fuel it could easily become too tail heavy if two big adults were in the back. This could make it climb too steeply, make it more challenging to fly at a constant altitude, and difficult to lower the nose. This was especially a concern for me since I only weighed about one-hundred-ten pounds (boat cushion included), and so my weight in the pilot's seat would not balance out any weight in the back. A severely overloaded or unbalanced airplane might not fly at all.

I had flown with passengers in the back before, but I had never been faced with the problem of having to quickly estimate my passenger's weights. I wasn't about to ask each person how much they weighed. I knew that any number they might provide would likely be more aspirational than accurate. I figured that I could estimate their weights and put the heaviest passenger in the front seat to reduce the weight in the back.

It's not like this was an uncommon issue for pilots. I had a friend who flew jet charter flights and who once had to tell former President George H.W. Bush that he needed to leave behind one of his trusted aides because of weight limits. Fortunately for my friend, Bush was a recipient of the Distinguished Flying Cross for his service as a pilot during World War II and understood the problem. He was gracious about it and left his supposedly least important aide to find another means of travel. For me, this problem was mostly theoretical until that day at the airshow.

My plan to strategically seat the passengers was thwarted when I was initially prevented from getting to my airplane by some overzealous volunteer security staff who didn't believe that I was a pilot—even when I showed them my pilot certificate. To be fair, at that time when a pilot received a new certificate it was just a flimsy carbon copy of a form typed out by the person doing the checkride. The official certificate, a plastic card with a picture of Orville and Wilbur Wright, took several weeks to arrive in the mail from the FAA headquarters in Oklahoma City. It must have looked like I had made a bad forgery of a pilot certificate.

By the time I found some male pilot friends to vouch for me so that I could get past security, the airport manager's wife had already started boarding a group of three passengers into the Skyhawk. Since she was not a pilot herself, she had not been concerned with where the passengers sat. The trio consisted of two older women who looked to weigh around two-hundred pounds each and a thinner gentleman with a guide cane for the visually impaired. I mentally calculated that our weight would be near the maximum limit but not over it, but to my dismay the two women were already buckled into the back seats. My only consolation was that I figured I could convince one of the ladies to sit in front where they would have the best view.

Yet when I leaned in to ask one of them to switch seats, both ladies explained in unison, "Oh, no. George always rides in the front seat next to the pilot when we go flying." *Really,* I thought, as I surreptitiously eyed the cane George was using to make his way into the airplane. Clearly, this was not about the view.

I tried again with a new tactic.

"Well, there will be more room for the cane in the back, and we wouldn't want it to interfere with the rudder pedals," I explained, hoping to appear safety conscious. I was a professional after all.

"George knows not to let his cane get in the way," one of the ladies explained. "We do this every year, and he *always* sits in front."

George now chimed in too, as he hoisted himself into the front seat and showed me how he could carefully stow his cane clear of the pedals. "I love being up front where all the action is," he said gleefully. *Indeed.*

Now this is where, as a professional, I should have explained the situation and asked for their help. I could have appealed to their experience as frequent fliers to get their cooperation in helping me solve the weight issue. I had no reason to think that anyone would have been upset, yet still I didn't speak up.

The accident data has consistently shown that exceeding weight and balance limitations causes accidents. During one recent eight-year period from 2008–2016, there were one-hundred-thirty-six accidents involving smaller general aviation airplanes where the cause was overloading the airplane or loading it out of balance. One-third of those accidents were fatal. Despite what I had learned during pilot training and demonstrated the day before, why couldn't I be like my friend and tell this George, who was not a former President of the United States, that he needed to switch seats? There was no excuse for my behavior, but I think that my self-imposed pressure to be accepted as a commercial pilot allowed me to rationalize my poor decision.

As I taxied out, I pondered what the story of the crash would look like on the front page of the local newspaper. The headline would read something like: *Female pilot kills three passengers one day after obtaining her commercial pilot's certificate.* I thought about how this would now become fodder for those who didn't think women should be flying airplanes. What I didn't do was change my mind. Instead, I prepared myself for flying a heavily loaded, tail-heavy airplane.

I adjusted something called a trim wheel all the way forward so I wouldn't need so much forward pressure on the flight control wheel or yoke to keep the nose down. This would help prevent the nose from prematurely lifting off the ground as we gained speed on takeoff. I used the longest runway so there was plenty of room to achieve liftoff despite our weight, and I reminded myself the airplane would be harder to fly smoothly with all the weight in the back. I decided to make a shallow climb after takeoff, and that on our return I would land without putting the flaps all the way down. All these precautions would reduce the chances of climbing at too steep of an angle and potentially stalling the airplane. I used all my aeronautical knowledge to adjust for my dumb decision to take off in the first place.

Despite taking these precautions, I wasn't prepared for what happened next. As we accelerated slowly and I ever so gently applied back pressure to the yoke, we leaped off the runway like a gazelle beginning a chase. Holding the yoke forward, my biceps got so shaky from the exertion that I had to lock my elbow against my body for added leverage. Rivulets of sweat ran down my face and I was relieved that my visually impaired passenger in the front couldn't see me struggling. George and his friends in the back were happily commenting on how much fun it was to be flying again when all I could think of was how much I wanted to be back on the ground. I immediately regretted my gutless decision as I made a shallow turn back toward the airport for landing. My only salvation was that my boss had told me to keep these flights as short as possible.

As I circled to set up for my landing, I pondered how I was

going to keep the tail from hitting the runway when I pulled the nose up for the landing flare. I didn't want to attract the attention of hundreds of airshow attendees with a loud bang and the sound of metal scraping the asphalt. As we floated over the runway, I left some power on instead of pulling the throttle back to idle. It prolonged the strain on my arm, but it lessened the chance of a hard landing. Just as I anticipated, as soon as I reduced the power by pulling back the throttle and released my elbow from where it was wedged into my ribs, the nose popped up and the wheels squeaked onto the runway. Somehow, I had managed to not scrape the tail. As I taxied in, relieved to be on the ground, the last thing I wanted to do was to pick up some more passengers. I felt like my commercial pilot's certificate deserved to be shredded.

As it was, there was a line of people waiting for me to take them for a ride. My first paying passengers were blissfully unaware of my lack of judgment. Although no one could have perceived a difference between the pilot that took off moments before, and the one that just landed, I knew I was not the same pilot. I now understood that a piece of paper that said I was a commercial pilot had nothing to do with being a professional.

A year later, I was asked to take people up for rides at the airshow again. As I stood by the airplane looking at the line of people ready to go up for a ride, some familiar faces caught my attention. It was George and his two companions. They recognized me too and were excited to go up for another ride. This time would be different. I was prepared to ask them to sit where I needed them to be for the weight and balance limitations and I had made sure that the airplane was not full of fuel. This year I would not just be a professional pilot. I would act like one.

Unable

I was sitting in the right seat of a Cessna-172, a popular four-seat, single-engine airplane, with a student I had just met. The student pilot to my left had completed his first solo flight the day before and was pursuing his bachelor's degree in flight operations. A timid college freshman, he barely made eye contact with me and gripped the throttle tightly with his sweaty right hand. He had done the rest of his flight training with a different instructor. This lesson was his first stage check—a periodic evaluation of his flying skills by an instructor other than his regular one. The flight program he was using for his training had a FAA requirement that this stage check be completed on the next flight after his first solo flight. It was sort of like getting a second opinion of his ability to continue flying safely on his own. Instead of getting to fly with his regular instructor, the one he had trusted with his life since he took his first lesson, he had to fly with me and prove that he didn't need any help from me.

Adding to his anxiety was the fact that this was the busiest time of day at this airport with its one runway that was associated with a college flight training program. There were six airplanes in front of us on the taxiway that led to the runway. Congestion and delays were a common problem, especially at this time of year between October and the Thanksgiving break. All the freshmen flight students were learning how to take off, land, and fly by themselves for the first time, so the airport and the sky surrounding it was jammed with airplanes that could have had the equivalent of a student driver sign in the window. The controller was talking faster than usual as he tried to get some airplanes out before others came in to land. To my student, I suspect the controller sounded like someone reading the disclaimers at the end of a car commercial.

As we slowly made our way to the front of the line for the runway, the student tentatively transmitted to the tower, "Cessna three zero four delta whiskey, ready for takeoff." Takeoffs are normally my favorite part of flying. Even after thousands of takeoffs, I am still in awe every time I look out the side window to see that the landing gear is no longer in contact with the ground. The process of becoming airborne continues to seem far-fetched to me, even though I now understand the physics behind the feat. It seems miraculous that air particles I can't see can be moved in a way to get us airborne. I think this respect I have for the triumph of becoming airborne is also a survival mechanism. Takeoffs are second only to landings as the most dangerous time during a flight. Flight instructors need to be particularly alert any time a new student is taking off, and even more so when that student is already feeling anxious.

As I expected, the controller came back with a rapid-fire reply to the student's transmission: "Cessna four delta whiskey, cleared for an immediate takeoff. Traffic on a two-mile final." By using the word "immediate" the controller was telling us not to dawdle because there was an airplane coming in for a landing on our runway that was two miles out. It meant that the controller expected us to taxi onto the runway without delay and to commence the takeoff without pausing on the runway. Experienced pilots are used to this, especially if they fly out of busy airports, but this was new to my student. His need to be methodical and purposeful as a novice was at odds with a controller who needed promptness in his effort to get us off the ground before another airplane landed. Often, a student pilot in this situation thinks only about complying with the takeoff clearance and not how to tell the controller that they can't do it safely. It's as if that disembodied voice in their headset is their drill sergeant and they are a new cadet. They rush through their takeoff despite having been trained that it's a pilot's responsibility to not follow any instructions they think will put them in an unsafe situation.

Like a harried commuter who floors the gas pedal as soon as a traffic light turns green, my timid but compliant student shoved the throttle forward, throwing me against the flimsy-feeling door as he made the ninety-degree left turn onto the runway. Our tires skidded across the asphalt as we accelerated. We overshot the turn so that instead of seeing the white lines of the runway centerline out the front windshield, I saw we were headed off the side of the runway. He stomped on the left rudder pedal to keep us from careening off the right side of the runway. We narrowly missed hitting a runway light. I had no choice but to fix this debacle, either by getting us off the ground before we ended up in the trees or by aborting the takeoff by pulling back the throttle. Given that we had another airplane right behind us trying to land, like having a tractor trailer tailgating you, I decided the safest course of action was to take the controls away from him and get us off the ground.

Often the problem in situations like this is that new student pilots have just begun to learn the jargon that allows them to say things succinctly over the radio and sound like a pilot; the thought of deviating from this limited repertoire of words to explain themselves in plain English seems sacrilegious. Talking to a controller over the radio is like a form of public speaking, able to be heard by pilots or controllers listening on the same radio frequency. Now pilots have an even bigger audience for any fumbles they make on the radio as there are sites on the internet where you can listen to live or recorded radio transmissions between pilots and controllers. The pressure to perform on the radio can add to the stress and make a novice pilot rush to acknowledge the instructions even as they know it's a bad idea. I had seen the consequences of rushing many times. In their haste, students have taken off with a window still open, or their seatbelt straps caught in the door, or with objects left unsecured on the dashboard—and those are just the ones that have flown with me.

For situations like this, pilots need to learn the power of the word "unable." Outside of aviation, this word implies a lack of agency, a way of saying I can't. For a pilot, it represents the opposite—it's a way for a pilot to tell a controller *I won't be doing that because it's unsafe* using only one word. It reinforces the reality that only a pilot knows their abilities and limitations as well as those of their airplane and so only they can determine whether it's safe to comply with any clearance. This was an important concept for this student to learn, but first I had to get us safely away from the ground.

As I took over the flight controls by telling him *My airplane,* I could sense his despair. He looked defeated, like he was expecting to be told he was not cut out to be a pilot. I knew that look and the fear he felt because I had been in that situation as a new student pilot. So, when this student and I were at a safe altitude and distance from the airport, I asked him to recall what it felt like the day before when he flew the airplane by himself. As his grip relaxed on the yoke, I explained how the word "unable" was key to communicating with the tower. By just saying this one word in reply to the controller's instructions, he could quickly convey that he needed more time and couldn't make an immediate takeoff. Then I told him to fly the airplane like I wasn't there. This was not an easy task given the cramped cockpit that left us bumping knees and elbows. Yet, it was necessary if I was going to be able to determine if he was safe to fly by himself again.

Some instructors might have ended the stage check as soon as the student made his botched attempt to take off. They would have sent him back to his instructor who would supposedly teach him not to make this mistake again. But this wasn't the kind of issue where he needed more instruction in a specific flying skill like say, doing crosswind landings. This was an error in judgment prompted by his lack of experience. Now that he had seen firsthand the consequences of a rushed takeoff and knew how to assert his authority as the pilot of this airplane, he would not likely make this mistake again. This authority of the pilot to do what is necessary to keep the flight safe is so fundamental to flying that they even refer to the pilot who is in charge as the "pilot in command." What he most needed now was a chance to restore the confidence he had felt the day before when he left his instructor on the ground and flew the airplane by himself.

Whenever you have an instructor flying with you, there is always some doubt about whether they helped you land the airplane. Sometimes even an instructor who is seemingly mute has inadvertently helped the student with the smallest of gestures. One student pilot I flew with let it slip that he knew when to raise the nose for the landing flare when he saw the index finger on my right hand start to twitch. A student pilot only knows for certain that they did all the flying themselves when they look to their right, and no one is there. That is the feeling he needed to recapture.

I couldn't help but recall that when I soloed for the first time, the sense of agency I gained from that experience empowered me to not only fly the airplane but to also deal with some issues on the ground that had nothing to do with flying airplanes. My biology teacher in both middle school and high school (he transferred to the high school when I got there—to my dismay) was a sadistic and twisted man who had a plausible reason for maintaining a closet full of formaldehyde-soaked creatures and their body parts. He forced me to stay after school nearly every day to clean specimen jars filled with such things as a cow's heart, a sheep's eye, and a dead cat with her stillborn kittens. All the while he would stand in the doorway of the closet, blocking my way out, telling me no one was going to stop him from doing anything he liked. Although he never touched me, the implication that he could was always there. I was terrified of him and did whatever he asked of me because he threatened to flunk me if I refused. Recognizing that my grades were important to me, he waved my lab reports and drawings in front of the class (and in front of my sister who sat in the front row) while telling the entire class that I was going to flunk while Sherry was going to get all A's.

It was so bad that one day we were supposed to be drawing pictures of the hydras that we observed on a slide under our microscopes when Sherry said to me in a panicked whisper that she had dropped her hydra on the floor. I was meticulously trying to draw my hydra and was planning on surreptitiously giving my slide to her when time ran out. The next day he held up the drawing of a hydra she had made from copying it out of her textbook. Her paper had a big red "A" at the top. Then he held up my carefully rendered drawing of my hydra with a big "C-" on it. "Now here is what a hydra looks like," he bellowed while holding Sherry's paper up high, telling me that I would again have to stay after and clean jars in his closet for extra credit.

After enduring this through middle school, and then having it start all over again in high school, it was clear that I was on my own to deal with this. No one, not my parents or other teachers who knew what was going on were going to stand up to him and make it stop. Yet, things felt different as soon as I flew an airplane by myself for the first time. It was as if seeing that empty seat to my right and feeling how quickly the Cessna climbed without the added weight of my instructor had instantaneously made me feel like a superhero. After I had faced down that runway in front of me, that suddenly looked much shorter and narrower than before when my instructor was by my side, and feeling the wheels smoothly contact the ground once again, I was a new person. I confronted my biology teacher in front of the class when he began accusing me of cheating on a test on genetics. He had already announced to the class the day before that the test was going to be so challenging that not even I could pass it. What he didn't know was that I took that as a challenge to delve into the topic with such zeal that I ended up getting a perfect score on the test. Everyone else in the class got below a seventy. Now he was not only accusing me of cheating, but he also accused me of ruining the grading curve for everyone else.

"You must have cheated," he snarled from behind his big desk, the veins in his neck bulging and his balding head red and sweaty.

"No, I didn't cheat," I said, my mouth dry and my legs shaking.

"You must have cheated," he said again, "because some of these questions were not even covered in the textbook."

"Yes, I know," I said, "but I got some other books out of the library and studied those too. I like genetics."

He was dumbfounded that not only was I speaking up, but that he had let it slip that he had created an unfair test. My voice was shaking the whole time, but I knew I had him. He was a coward and a bully after all, and my fighting back made it no fun for him. He wanted to crush the life out of me like one of the decaying creatures in his closet, but now it was like I had suddenly developed claws to fight back. I had just flown an airplane by myself, and I was no longer going to be intimidated by him. That was the last time he singled me out for abuse.

As I watched this student pilot do several takeoffs and landings while communicating effectively with the controller and dealing with the practice emergency situations that I put him in, I was impressed with his transformation from an anxious student to confident pilot with each successful takeoff and landing that he made. He refused to be rushed, seemingly unable to let anything interfere with his focus on flying the airplane that was now at his command. He was ready now to learn new skills like how to navigate to other airports or fly at night, or perhaps how to better handle the challenges of being a freshman at a new college far away from home.

Baby Bumps

Before I became a parent, I was blissfully ignorant of how hard it would be to balance motherhood and flying airplanes. Part of the problem likely stemmed from the fact that I didn't know any active pilots who were mothers. I was working for a smaller airline in the Northeast, flying the Saab SF340B, and out of our eighty or so pilots there were six other female pilots including the chief pilot. Three were married, but they were all at an age that it was unlikely they were going to be starting families.

One of those single pilots was my roommate, and she soon married another pilot. I remember looking at photographs from her honeymoon in Hawaii and talking about how we both wanted a family. She talked about it like being pregnant and flying was as simple as remembering to pack your prenatal vitamins. Maybe she was as naive as I was. It was the first time I didn't feel like I was crazy to want to fly and be a mother.

At the time I was thinking about trying to get pregnant, I was close to having enough seniority to make captain. That would mean a big bump in pay, so the timing seemed right, along with the fact that I was quickly approaching thirty. Our airline had just opened a new base in Boston, which meant that I no longer had to commute to Burlington, Vermont, from New Hampshire for my trips. I was reporting to Boston's Logan International Airport at 5 in the morning Monday through Thursday for a 6 o'clock departure to Albany and Rochester, New York, and then back again. Barring any mechanical or weather-related delays, I was home by noon having missed all the notorious Boston traffic. I was so clueless that I thought this schedule would be perfect for a new mother and would allow me to nap alongside my baby in the afternoon. What could possibly go wrong?

I suspected right away that I was pregnant because I felt nauseous, much like I did during my first few flying lessons except I now felt that way before I had even gotten out of bed. It turned out a pregnant pilot was a new thing at my airline, and there were no guidelines about how long a pregnant pilot could continue to fly. I was so tired that I had to stop and rest three times on the way from the employee parking lot to our departure gate. To be fair I was caring two big bags, one for my clothes and one for all the manuals we had to carry with us. Flight attendants had just started using the bags with wheels, but I felt like I had to carry my bags like all the other pilots did. It was stupid. The chief pilot wisely suggested that I should consult an obstetrician right away to see if I should go on medical leave until I felt better. This baby was already kicking my butt.

While I was disappointed that the airline industry was still not prepared for dealing with a pregnant pilot, I wasn't surprised. Still, I was disillusioned when the obstetrician was equally unprepared for what advice to give a pregnant pilot. When I explained that I had questions about flying while pregnant she said, "Don't worry about it. That's why there are two pilots in case one passes out there is always a backup." I'm not sure what bothered me most about her comment—the fact that she thought one pilot did nothing but wait for the other one to keel over, or the fact she felt compelled to explain my job to me. I found another doctor.

The issue became moot two weeks later when my airline was sold and ceased operating with no notice. In retrospect we should have been able to predict that our airline was in desperate financial straits. The packages of cheese and crackers given to passengers suddenly became a tiny package of dry pretzels. Then even those went away along with the napkin that usually accompanied your choice of beverage. The thirty-four seats on our Saab were largely empty on at least half of the flights and often we flew with only one passenger. This was especially awkward because we had to ask that one passenger to sit in the very last seat by the lavatory to keep the airplane from becoming too nose heavy. Nothing inspires confidence in a small propeller-driven airplane, especially when the passenger thought they were going to be flying on a big jet, like the fact that the first officer just told you this airplane will only fly properly if you sit in a specific seat.

Despite these ominous signs that things were not financially well, we were all shocked because our airline had been bought and sold before and kept flying the same routes. On what turned out to be my last trip as a first officer in the Saab, I was just a few weeks pregnant and still suffering from morning sickness. The captain and I had to do a rare circling approach into Poughkeepsie, N.Y. A circling approach is just what it sounds like—a maneuver at the end of an instrument approach where you often must fly around the airport to line up with the landing runway instead of being set up going straight in. It was bumpy since we were just below the clouds, and I gulped and took deep breaths while trying to avoid puking into my headset's microphone. I finally admitted to the captain that I was not feeling well because I was pregnant, thinking that this news would keep him from worrying that I was afflicted with something more serious like food poisoning or appendicitis. It turned out that he was not thinking about my welfare at all. "Oh, great," he said glumly. My wife is pregnant, and I thought I was going to get a break from watching someone puke all the time.. I was exhausted and grouchy by the time we finally landed at Boston, and apparently so was my captain. After we turned onto the taxiway, a flirtatious controller asked me if I wanted to meet him at a local pub for a drink since we were both going off duty. Without hesitation, my captain pushed the tiny microphone button and said, "You're too late. She's already knocked up."

Now that I was no longer flying, there was nothing for me to do except wait for the birth of my first child while worrying about the loss of my health benefits and the job I loved. I still had to look for work to collect unemployment, so I sent out resumes to many other airlines. By the time I got an interview for another regional airline, I was too pregnant to conceal it. I told the recruiter on the phone that I was pregnant and would be happy to interview for a start date later in the year when they would be running another ground school. To my disappointment the recruiter abruptly ended the call, saying they were no longer interested in talking to me—as if my being a mother somehow made me unqualified even though nothing had changed about my flight experience or desire to fly. The recruiter clearly had made a presumption about my willingness and ability to return to flying after becoming a mother. Maybe I should have just shown up for the interview without divulging what would be obvious upon my arrival, but I didn't think being pregnant was going to affect anything except my possible start date. It was as if they thought being pregnant was a permanent medical condition that prevented you from ever flying again.

It was also challenging because I was not used to having so much free time on my hands. I was probably in the best shape of my life because I joined a water aerobics class for pregnant mothers, and I worked out at the YMCA nearly every day. I was hoping to have an easy delivery (doesn't every first-time mother want that and think it's within their control somehow), and I read about all the ways that being fit can help when you are in labor. I didn't run a marathon or anything like that, but I did a lot of yoga and strength training, and I felt great for the last six months of my pregnancy.

I had taught myself how to sew the previous year when I was on call for the airline a lot of the time and had to remain close to home. My sewing hobby came in handy when I got pregnant because there were not as many options as there are today for maternity clothes. I was used to shopping for clothes at second-hand stores to save money, but I couldn't find any options for used maternity wear. Sewing maternity clothes was a perfect solution since I wasn't skilled at adjusting patterns to fit properly and that was not an issue. If something I made was too big, I knew I would grow into it. I guess you could say that I was nesting because I also began making baby clothes. For someone like me who had been so focused on my career, it was a nice change of pace, but I missed flying and wished I knew at least one other pilot who was also a mother.

When my pregnancy dragged on past my due date, I wasn't too concerned. I even went to the YMCA to walk on the treadmill several days after my due date. When a young male staffer asked me when the baby was due, he turned ashen when I told him nonchalantly that I was five days overdue and that I hoped some exercise might get things moving along. With the increased circulation that comes with pregnancy, my face would also turn crimson with even the slightest amount of exertion. I really freaked out that poor guy.

Christina was born on a Saturday at lunchtime, and although I had very little experience with babies, I could tell right away that my daughter was a force to be reckoned with. I had heard some parents describe newborns and young babies as boring because all they do is sleep, eat, and poop. Perhaps their babies were just not as fascinating as mine. I didn't sleep most of the first night after Christina was born, not because she was crying, but because I didn't want to miss anything. My daughter's personality was evident from the start. I say this because she engaged in a battle with the nursing assistant who kept swaddling her very tightly just like I used to make my mother do with my favorite doll and blanket. Despite what the books said about how newborns like to have their arms and legs cocooned against their bodies, this didn't apply to Christina. As soon as the nursing assistant left the room, as if she was waiting for her to be out of sight, Christina would start grunting and wriggling until she got herself out of that blanket. Only then would she relax and go to sleep. The third time the nursing assistant appeared in my room to re-swaddle my baby, I told her to find another newborn to swaddle because mine clearly didn't like it. The nursing assistant scolded me in a condescending tone, saying that she knew what was best for my baby. I surprised myself when I kicked her out of my room. I was thrilled that my daughter had strong opinions already.

As it turned out, the early 1990s was not a great time to be looking for a job as a pilot. Aviation has always been a cyclical profession, and events in the world can squash the need for pilots in an instant. Pilot shortages have also been predicted many times, but in 1992 when I was ready to return to flying, nearly every pilot I knew was furloughed or unemployed. One of my friends had been hired and furloughed from six different airlines before he managed to get hired at Delta. One time he had just finished ground school when his new airline furloughed him before he ever got a chance to fly the new airplane he had spent weeks learning.

I had always wanted to have children that were close in age as I had enjoyed having a constant playmate in my twin (most of the time). For both of those reasons, it seemed like the right time to have another child. I was also going to be turning thirty, and that number triggered in me a feeling not unlike a caution light in an airplane. While the demand for pilots was cyclical, biology dictated that my prospects of having another healthy child would only diminish with age. I also wanted to continue to breastfeed Christina for a while and that seemed like an impossibility if I returned to flying right away. Over three decades later, few of the airlines have clear policies accommodating breastfeeding for pilots and flight attendants. I can't tell you the number of times that I saw breasts displayed on calendars in the maintenance bays and in offices at the airport where the mostly male ground crews worked, but policies that allow breasts to be used for their intended purpose have been slow to emerge. Maybe if more women were in upper management the airlines would not need to be reminded of the real purpose of breasts.

My second daughter, Ashley, was born twenty-one months after her sister. There had been no signs of a problem during my pregnancy except for some concern, mostly on my part, that she wasn't moving very much. Whereas Christina had been a real kicker, Ashley was sedate, but every afternoon I was reassured when she would start moving because she had the hiccups. The obstetrician even showed me during an ultrasound how she was sucking her thumb and twitching every few seconds with each hiccup. I was delighted by this and thought perhaps it was a good omen that she would be a better sleeper than her colicky sister had been.

The ultrasounds showed that Ashley was smaller than her sister, even though I didn't go into labor until forty-two weeks, and so the doctor was baffled as to why my labor was not progressing after twenty-four hours. As her heart rate started to drop, I was rushed to the operating room for an emergency cesarean. I insisted that I wanted to be awake so as not to miss a moment of her new life—which turned out to be a bad decision. I started vomiting at precisely the moment I needed to be still. After a few seconds of debate between the anesthesiologist who didn't want to give me too much anti-nausea medication, and the obstetrician who said that he couldn't get a baby out with me puking all the time, the obstetrician won out. I was very groggy, but I got to see Ashley's beet red face before falling asleep.

When I woke up back in my room, an orthopedic surgeon was standing at my bedside. Ashley had been born with a left foot that was severely twisted in what is known as a clubfoot. The orthopedist assured me that serial casting for six months followed by surgery would make her foot functional for walking. He was careful to say that it would never be quite the same as her right foot, but that it shouldn't hold her back unless she was hoping to be an Olympic sprinter.

I sobbed the next day as I watched the orthopedist smear a pasty white concoction around her tiny foot and leg, all the way up to her knee. As it hardened into a cast, I couldn't help thinking how unfair it was that my daughter already had a limitation placed on her on her second day of life. What if she wanted to be an Olympic sprinter? I suspect the doctor thought my tears were the result of hormonal changes, but he was kind and reassuring without denying that her foot would never be perfect. He knew how concerned I was because I had walked from my room at the other end of the hallway without any help to be there when the cast was put on. It was just hours after the cesarean delivery, when apparently most mothers right out of surgery haven't gotten out of bed yet. At least that is what they told me when they offered (more like insisted) that I take a wheelchair ride back to my room.

What I didn't tell anyone was that this pregnancy felt precarious from the start, like an uneasy feeling that I might have a miscarriage. I had no such feelings with my firstborn, so it didn't add up that I would be more concerned the second time around. I had nothing to base this feeling on, but it was pervasive throughout my pregnancy. I relaxed a bit after the first trimester, but I still had a feeling that this baby was somehow needier than her sibling.

As a pilot, I had taught my students not to ignore gut feelings that something is wrong while they are flying. I had developed an early interest in how pilots process information and make decisions, and I knew that we process some of the information we get through our senses on a subconscious level, often feeling like something is amiss before we can articulate what might be causing this feeling. That is why people often report feeling uneasy right before something dramatic happens. For a pilot, paying attention to this feeling can prompt them to be more attentive and to see something that they otherwise might have missed. Knowing this, I figured that my slight unease during the pregnancy might have been because something indescribable was going on that was different from my first pregnancy. Now that I could see Ashley, instead of just a blurry image on a computer screen, I noticed things that seemed to concern only me. At least no one else was telling me that they were concerned even if maybe they were. Did she only have a club foot and nothing else unusual going on?

While Christina had burst onto the scene already opinionated about being swaddled, Ashley was intolerant in a different way. Ashley seemed to be overwhelmed by many of the sights, sounds, and textures around her, rather than annoyed at any one thing. Even though I was on pain medication and recovering from the surgery, I still could clearly see that Ashley wasn't doing some of the things that Christina had done at birth. When I leaned Ashley back into a position so she could breastfeed, she didn't react the way that Christina had done and which I later learned was called the Moro reflex. When newborns are moved in a way where they feel unsupported, like when you lean them backward so they can latch on to breastfeed, they will flail their arms out to the side as if in a panic. Instead, when I leaned her back, Ashley remained floppy in my arms. At one point I even demonstrated for the nurse, leaning her back and then bringing her forward over and over. The nurse gave me a look that said she thought I was a crazy new mother.

The next day I thought sure the pediatrician who was sent in to see Ashley for her first newborn visit would have something to say about how thin she looked. She weighed two pounds less than Christina did at birth and yet she was the same length. Ashley looked like she had not grown into her body. I didn't express any concerns to him after being dismissed by the nurse, but I watched him intently to see if he offered anything to relieve my anxiety. I remember the pediatrician looking into Ashley's mouth and saying that she had a high arched palate. Was that a bad thing? Sensing my concern, he looked in my mouth and said that I also had an oddly shaped palate. Was this supposed to be comforting? Do babies inherit their parent's palates like they do their eyes and nose? At one point the pediatrician even remarked that Ashley looked a bit jaundiced—the yellowish color of the skin and the whites of the eyes that is common among newborns. Then he looked at me. "Her skin color is a lot like yours," he said. *Wait, what? Doesn't that make me jaundiced too?* This pediatrician had an explanation for everything even if some of them didn't make sense.

When I reflect on this experience now, I wonder if the pediatrician's attempt to explain away everything that seemed off was due to something called confirmation bias. I learned about this phenomenon through my training as a pilot. Confirmation bias is the tendency to notice things that support what we already think is true and to seek evidence that we are right. For a pilot it may cause them to ignore evidence that the weather is deteriorating faster than forecasted because they don't want to accept that they must turn around or land short of their destination. Or they might convince themselves the airport they see is the one they are looking for even if there are many indications that they are incorrect. For Ashley's pediatrician, confirmation bias might have led him to find reasons why she was like me rather than acknowledging signs of genetic abnormalities he didn't want to be true. Perhaps he didn't want to be the bearer of bad news. Whatever the reason, my concerns about Ashley were dismissed.

At the same time, I was experiencing my own symptoms that were not typical of someone who had just delivered a child. I was having severe pain in my upper back, particularly near my right shoulder blade, and I continued to feel nauseous. Every time a nurse came in, I told her about this pain and was told it was likely gas pain from the surgery. Gas pain in my upper back made no sense to me, and when one nurse reminded me that it was normal for my incision to hurt, I said that I didn't feel pain anywhere near my incision. I began to feel like I was losing my mind.

After four days in the hospital, I was feeling worse and more dismissed than ever. I was unable to eat anything without feeling nauseous. While Ashley's skin color was nearly back to normal, I could see my eyes were still yellow in the bathroom mirror. The pain in my back now affected the whole right side of my abdomen. I was sent home with my newborn and Christina to take care of despite it all. After two days at home, I couldn't get out of bed without help. Finally, I saw my obstetrician again and enough time had passed since giving birth that he knew something else must be causing the pain. When I gingerly pointed to a spot on the right side of my abdomen not anywhere near my incision as the source of the pain, it came to him that I was having a gallbladder attack.

Apparently, it is not uncommon to develop gallbladder issues while pregnant, and when I was admitted back to the same wing of the hospital I had just left, one of the nurses said, "Oh, of course. Now it makes perfect sense." Besides the pain near a shoulder blade, another symptom of a gallbladder attack is jaundice. This is why my pallor was the same as my jaundiced newborn. All the signs were there indicating a gallbladder attack, but because of the baby and the Cesarean birth, everyone was focused on that and ignored signs telling them that something else was wrong. One week after Ashley was born, I had my gallbladder removed. As the anesthesiologist held the oxygen mask over my face, about to put me to sleep, he said, "Oh, I remember you! You were the Momma who was puking when the obstetrician was trying to get the baby out!"

"Yup," I mumbled sleepily. "That was me."

During the first six months after Ashley was born, I kept asking her pediatrician why she wasn't doing the same things her older sister had done. I had all of Christina's milestones recorded in her baby book and nothing but blank lines in Ashley's book. Each time I brought up my concerns, I was told to just wait and see. Even though I wasn't flying now, I couldn't help but compare the way that pilots are taught to deal with issues raised in an airplane to how doctors were handling my concerns about my daughter. As pilots we are taught when there is an issue that may affect the safety of the flight that we must continually update the information we are receiving and monitor the status of that issue. For example, if we are preparing to takeoff and snow has been removed from the wings, we are required to keep checking to make sure the wings remain clear up to the point when we start the takeoff. It seemed like my pediatrician, and even the nurses in the hospital, both dismissed concerns I had raised about Ashley and my own condition without checking in to see if things had changed. I was sent home with no further information gathered on my increasing pain, and no tests were ordered for Ashley even though she was rapidly losing weight.

It wasn't until Ashley began being treated for her clubfoot in a different hospital that saw many children with genetic conditions that things began to change. A nurse who worked in the room where Ashley got her new casts every few weeks began to question me about her development. As she watched Christina gracefully running around the sparse casting room, she kept asking me if Ashley was doing the same things that Christina had done at the same age. When I admitted that I was worried and that no one was listening to me, she left the room and returned with an appointment card for a genetics clinic. "This is where you need to go if you want answers," she said. This nurse had kept checking in with me and monitoring the situation with Ashley, and much like an experienced pilot might recognize an issue that a novice might miss, this nurse had the right experience to recognize a problem.

In the decades since then, the staff who work in operating rooms in hospitals have started utilizing some of the same safety policies and procedures that pilots have used for many years to reduce the number of errors. They now use checklists like pilots do and they even pause right before they begin a surgery to confirm that everyone is ready to go and on the same page—much like a takeoff briefing. I wonder if I my experience with Ashley might have been different if it happened today. It also makes me wonder if the medical profession will ever move toward more open investigations when a serious error occurs like the way that the National Transportation Safety Board holds open hearings when there is an accident. In the medical field, bad patient outcomes are discussed in private conferences behind closed doors which leaves fewer opportunities to learn from the mistakes of others.

Things happened quickly after Ashley's genetic testing was complete, but the confidence I felt in an airplane disappeared when dealing with the many new medical professionals that entered our lives. Her genetic abnormality on chromosome one was so rare that there were no other cases to read about. I wanted to dive into manuals like I had in ground school and learn everything about Ashley's condition, but that wasn't possible. One pediatric resident confided that in medical school the lecture on chromosome one abnormalities consisted solely of a statement from the professor that this diagnosis was "incompatible with life." Then they moved on. There was nothing more to say. No wonder this resident looked like he had seen a ghost when I assured him that Ashley had an extra piece of genetic material on her first chromosome.

The neurologist who examined Ashley's brain scans was not optimistic that she would ever walk, talk, or achieve any meaningful level of education. Portions of her corpus callosum, the part of the brain that joins the left and right halves of the brain together, were missing. The medical profession has its own acronyms and terminology, much like in aviation, and it was all so unfamiliar to me. I remember reading the radiologist's report on Ashley's scans and seeing the words "cerebral atrophy." When I looked up the definition of atrophy, I started shaking as I read that it referred to a "wasting away." I thought it meant that Ashley's brain was progressively getting smaller, and that terrified me. Yet I was also scared to ask the question about whether Ashley's condition was going to get worse or not.

When your family and friends learn you have given birth to a baby with genetic differences, they want to comfort you by sharing things they think will help. I soon received a copy of an essay written by Emily Perl Kingsley called "Welcome to Holland." In the piece Kingsley compares finding out your child has a disability to planning for a flight to Italy, and then finding out you have landed in Holland instead. Kingsley describes how you will always be wistful about your planned trip to Italy, meaning the planned birth of your child, but that over time you will come to recognize that Holland, or the birth of your child with a disability, is a beautiful destination too. As with many things, some parents find comfort in this essay, while others argue that it fails to acknowledge the serious demands of raising a child with disabilities. I understood how people who knew me might think this essay, with its analogy to flying, would suit me. When I read this, I began to sob, but not for the reasons I think the author of the poem intended. I couldn't help but wonder if my new reality meant that flying anywhere was going to be impossible for me. I cared little about the destination—only the flying itself.

Even after Ashley's diagnosis, interactions with the many medical professionals I needed to communicate with were difficult. Often, I would see that someone had changed the diagnosis I had recorded on Ashley's medical history to Down syndrome, a far more common genetic disorder than Ashley's, but unrelated to it. It was especially difficult to go from being someone who was entrusted with the lives of an airplane full of people to someone who was not considered a reliable source of information on her own daughter's genetic condition. I missed flying, but I also missed the sense of control that flying gave me. Everything about this situation seemed out of my control. The one thing I did that felt right was I switched pediatricians. In the process of doing that I got a copy of my daughter's medical records. That was how I found out that the pediatrician had made a note prior to Ashley's diagnosis that "mother is hyper-attentive to Ashley's development." How could I be too attentive?

Those first few years of Ashley's life were more stressful than anything I had been through as a pilot. Like a flight attendant who must appear calm for the passengers even when things are going wrong, I had to hide my worry about Ashley's health in front of Christina. I wanted her to have as normal a life as possible despite the many trips to the hospital for Ashley's bouts of pneumonia, the surgery on her clubfoot, and a tonsillectomy that left her with a blood infection that she nearly did not survive. To make up for it, I took Christina to gymnastics classes, and when she got tired of that I signed her up for dance classes with her friends. Just as Christina sat through all the doctors' appointments, Ashley would sit patiently on my lap while Christina took tap and ballet class and twirled around in her blue tutu. I admit that sometimes it was hard to sit in the waiting room of the dance studio with the other mothers who had children Ashley's age and be reminded of all the things Ashley couldn't do yet.

One day I was sitting in a room filled with dance trophies waiting for Christina to finish her tap lesson. Ashley was again sitting in my lap sucking her thumb while a few boys were chasing each other around the room while waiting for their sisters. Ashley was nearly two but still couldn't sit by herself or speak any words. She was intently watching everyone around her. She took her thumb out for only a moment to wave and smile at one of the boys who had made a funny face for her. When the boys heard a train whistle, they noisily ran outside to watch it. That left only two mothers and a girl, probably about six, left sitting in the room with Ashley and me. I was lost in thought when one of the mothers leaned over and said, "How nice that your daughter sits so quietly on your lap." I wanted to scream and tell her how it really was, to watch the other children and wonder if Ashley would ever be able to walk or talk like them, or dance like her sister. I wanted to say it wasn't such a wonderful thing to have a quiet child—that toddlers are supposed to be loud and run out the door to see a train.

As I sat there feeling envious of those other two mothers, the young girl came and sat down in front of Ashley and me. She started talking to Ashley, and the girl seemed not to be bothered that this was a one-sided conversation. Ashley smiled at her while continuing to suck her thumb. Then the girl looked up at me and asked, "Can she walk?" When I replied that she could not, the girl said, "That's okay. My little brother over there can't suck his thumb the way she can." That little girl's remark struck me in a way that nothing else had since I got Ashley's diagnosis. That girl made me realize that Ashley was not struggling with the unknown of her diagnosis—only I was, and maybe it was time to stop and enjoy Ashley for the gleeful child she already was and for what she might accomplish in her own time frame.

From the Cockpit to the Cadaver

After having spent more than half of my life flying airplanes, I now couldn't imagine returning to the nomadic life of an airline pilot. Ashley's needs were often unpredictable, but I was also concerned about how Christina was being impacted by the new demands on my time and energy. Christina was, in many ways, the perfect antidote to the seemingly endless worry about Ashley. The embodiment of precociousness, she started talking in complete sentences not long after her first birthday and was as agile as her sister was off balance. After my childhood spent feeling like only half of a matched pair, I knew how important it was for her to get some of my undivided attention.

Around this same time, I was offered a scholarship to attend a weekend conference for parents and caregivers of children with disabilities. I almost turned it down because it was on the same day as Ashley's first birthday, but I decided this was something I needed to attend. I was beginning to understand that holidays, especially birthdays, with Ashley brought lots of mixed emotions. On the one hand it was a time to celebrate, but it also was a reminder of all the milestones she was missing. It was an emotional time, and I needed to be around other parents who understood my complicated feelings of both joy and despair.

Part of me was also hopeful that somewhere in this beautiful location in the Blue Ridge Mountains of western North Carolina that someone would have the answers I was seeking about what my new profession should look like and how to get there. I still wanted to fly again, but I could no longer have my bag packed all the time except the one I kept packed for emergency trips to the hospital with Ashley. As I pondered the list of educational offerings, I saw one that intrigued me. I have long forgotten the catchy name of the session, but I concluded its description of helping parents learn how to let go of the dreams they once had for their lives and their child, and how to create new ones, was directed at me.

I admit I was dubious of how a ninety-minute session could make much of an impact on my struggle to find my path forward. Still, I was drawn by curiosity to that hotel conference room with about thirty people sitting in folding chairs. Surely none of these attendees, nearly all mothers like me, had been faced with giving up a flying career. In my delusional state of self-pity, mixed with a large amount of righteous anger at the many people who had made me question my own judgment as a parent, it never occurred to me there were other parents making equally tough choices. I took a seat at the end of a row, in case I needed to make a quick escape, and wondered what they intended to do with the yellow balloons filled with helium and tied with long strings to chairs at the front of the room.

One of the presenters introduced them both as mothers of young children who were born unexpectedly with disabilities. Then one of them started asking the parents to shout out the dreams that were lost the moment they learned their child had been born with a birth defect. One mother shouted that her daughter would never need the wedding dress that she was going to make her. And with that one of the presenters took a pin and popped one of those balloons. *Pop!* Another mother said that her son, who used a wheelchair, would never be able to play Little League baseball. *Pop!* Still another said her child would not need the college fund that she had already started for him. *Pop!* By the time three balloons had been popped, I was sobbing.

Then the presenters asked what dreams of our own we had given up to care for the child that needed so much more than we ever imagined. Someone said that they had to give up their dream of going back to college. *Pop!* Another said that they would have to forego buying their first home due to all the added expenses. *Pop!* No one mentioned giving up their career as an airline pilot, and I was too choked up to say it either, but silently I grieved the loss of my flying career and the dream that Ashley and Christina would play hours of catch or race each other on scooters as I had with my twin sister. I grieved the fact that with each new year the gap between them would widen as Christina moved through all the typical stages of growing up while Ashley remained a much younger child.

Then the presenters led us through their own experiences and how they were able to develop new dreams in light of their unexpected entrance into the world of disability. As they talked about how they learned to imagine new goals, each of us was given a new balloon and a piece of paper to write down a new dream for our child or ourselves. Then, they helped us brainstorm how to tackle the steps necessary to achieve that new goal.

By then I had become friendly with Ashley's physical therapist who came to our home twice a week to work on strengthening Ashley's muscles and improving her balance. I was fascinated with learning about how the body works and how I could use that knowledge to help Ashley and other children like her. As a pilot, I had also developed an interest in the field of aviation human factors: a field of study that explores how the relationship between aviation professionals such as pilots, controllers, and aerospace engineers, and the environments they work in, like cockpits and radar rooms, affect human performance. The field of aviation human factors includes such issues as the impact of cockpit design on pilot errors, the best ways to present air traffic information to controllers, and how to design better instrument panels to reduce pilot fatigue. Human factors have taken on added significance in aviation as accidents are increasingly due to human errors versus mechanical malfunctions. Although traditionally physical therapists work with children and adults to help them overcome physical challenges, I could also foresee an opportunity where what I would learn about anatomy, physiology, and ergonomics could be applied to issues in the field of aviation. Ideally, this could help me to both work with children with disabilities like my daughter, and to one day do research and teach as an aviation human factors expert. Although it seemed like an insurmountable goal to return to graduate school, I began at this session to write down the steps to gaining admission to a graduate program in physical therapy with these two goals in mind.

It would take me three years to complete the additional science classes in physics, chemistry, and biology that were prerequisites for physical therapy school. To be competitive for admission to a program I also needed some experience working in the medical field. I ended up taking a night class to become a nursing assistant and then spent six months working shifts at a local hospital on the orthopedic ward. Only then was I prepared to apply to graduate programs where statistically I had a one in four chance of being accepted. I applied to six schools and waited anxiously for the decisions knowing that wherever I ended up would be the place where Ashley would need to attend a preschool and where Christina would be in the first grade.

I was thrilled when I was accepted at the University of North Carolina. Besides having a highly ranked physical therapy school,

I could receive in-state tuition and have Ashley attend an innovative preschool program where she would be in an environment with typically developing peers and other children like her with a variety of disabilities. I also quickly learned that I needed to study up on basketball if I was going to be a Tarheel. My first week of class I was informed that I was an embarrassment to my new school when I remarked to a fellow student that I thought it was cool they named the Dean Dome in honor of all the deans at the university. (Of course, I now know it was named for the Tarheels basketball coach, Dean Smith).

Christina was six and Ashley was four when we moved to Chapel Hill, North Carolina, so that I could attend the two-year master's program there. The physical therapy program was located within the medical school which was attached to the hospital—a fact that would turn out to be fortuitous for both Ashley and me. Ashley would end up in the emergency room on the second day we were there. I began my first semester feeling decidedly out of place, but this was not new to me. This time I felt conspicuous not because of my gender but because my classmates were all high achievers, and many had worked in the healthcare field for years. They were fluent in the language of medicine like I was with aviation jargon.

One of the first classes we were required to take was one that had weeded out many potential healers—gross anatomy. Although the word "gross" was a fitting descriptor of some of the unpleasantness associated with this class which included cadaver dissection, the word was actually a reference to the fact that this was the study of body parts big enough that they could be seen without the aid of a microscope. After about a week of gross anatomy, I longed for the drone of the cockpit and wondered how in the world I ever thought I was cut out for this. I studied for my first gross anatomy exam inside an oxygenated tent attached to Ashley's hospital bed as she struggled to recover from yet another bout of pneumonia. For the first time in my life, I knew what it was like to get the worst grade in the class on an exam. On a multiple-choice test, I managed to get thirty-three percent of the questions right.

I thought the medical field, especially physical therapy, might give me a reprieve from some of the gender bias that persists in aviation. After all, of the forty students in my class, only six were male and the profession itself is overwhelmingly female. So, I was surprised at what happened when I admitted to the teaching assistant that my abysmal score on the first exam might be due in part to having to memorize diagrams from the *Atlas of Human Anatomy* while sleeping with Ashley in an oxygen tent. She had been tipped off by one of my classmates who had been concerned that my spot in the class could be in jeopardy if I didn't explain my situation. My new classmates, rather than being competitive with each other, were always looking out for me and each other, and it made what happened next even more disturbing in many ways.

The teaching assistant agreed that I needed to tell the professor for the class, an intimidating man who appeared to be well into his seventies and who had taught anatomy for the medical school for over half a century, the reason why I might have performed so poorly. I think she thought that he might give me a chance to retake the test, or at least would consider the situation when it came to my final grade if my scores improved. We both could not have been more wrong. When I reluctantly told the professor my circumstances, he said, "It sounds like you should drop out and focus on what should be your top priority—being a mother." The teaching assistant was so unused to such blatant sexism that I had to convince her not to quit her job on the spot. Sadly, I was used to this and once again I would have to prove myself.

I ran into another obstacle when we were tested using the various cadavers that we carefully dissected in the lab each week. For this portion of our exams, we were given a sheet of paper with spaces numbered 1–20 and a clipboard. Each student began the exam at a different table where a cadaver sat with tiny pieces of paper with a number pinned to various body parts. At each station we had a minute to write down the name, nerve supply, and function of the body part where the numbered pin was located. Sometimes the body parts were muscles like the piriformis or gastrocnemius, and other times the pins were inserted into valves of the heart or an internal organ like a gallbladder. Despite spending extra hours on the weekend in the cadaver lab memorizing various parts of human anatomy, and sometimes getting freaked out when I realized I was alone in a room full of cadavers holding an eyeball in my hand, each time I took one of these tests I would start shaking and feeling faint. All the hours of studying seemed to vanish in a flash as my mind went blank. This not only made it impossible to pass the tests, but it was also a source of embarrassment for me since, as a pilot and flight instructor, I prided myself on my ability to stay calm under stress.

Clearly, I couldn't go to my professor again and explain that I was having these odd symptoms, and I wasn't sure what they were about. I finally went to my advisor for the program, a seasoned professor who taught many of the pediatric classes that I enjoyed the most. Although she wasn't an experienced mental health counselor, she was the perfect person for me to confide in. As we sat there, she had me close my eyes and describe what happened as I imagined myself taking a test in the lab. I described how I went into a fight or flight response with my heart pounding, my focus narrowed, and a feeling like I was being suffocated. When she asked me if I had ever felt like this before, I shakily admitted that it felt like I was back in that specimen-filled closet while my biology teacher blocked the door back in middle and high school.

I later learned that the sense of smell is the one that most effectively brings back memories. It made sense that the smells in the cadaver lab brought me back to those traumatic times because some of the same chemicals that were used to preserve a cow's heart for biology class were used to preserve the cadavers we dissected. I ended up working with a mental health counselor on strategies to bring myself back to a feeling of calm and competence during those tests. It turned out that the image I focused on to calm myself during exams was of flying by myself on a night takeoff where the horizon was lit up by the setting sun. I managed to pass gross anatomy using the counselor's strategies. Once again, flying airplanes had helped me get through a challenging situation.

Despite all the fascinating things I was learning, it often seemed like I was crazy to attempt graduate school with a six-year-old and a four-year-old. I wrote papers late at night when the girls were asleep, but memorizing the twelve cranial nerves and the names of all the bones in the human body often had to be done while I was chauffeuring the girls to various appointments and activities. Ashley had also become adept at getting my attention despite being largely non-verbal. She was still getting around by scooting on her butt when one afternoon I kept hearing the familiar sound of her pants rubbing across the carpet as she scooted back and forth between the living room and her bedroom. I was trying to focus on writing a paper that I had failed to finish the night before. When I finally looked down to see what she was doing, she was naked and her bathing suit, towel, swim fins, sunscreen, and water shoes were all piled up next to my chair. I stopped what I was doing, and we went to the pool. Ashley was finding ways to communicate with me even if she had to use different methods. I thought her creativity and tenacity were both signs of her intelligence and ability to problem solve and it gave me hope for her future even if it was sometimes inconvenient to drop everything and go to the pool.

By my second year of graduate school, I was looking forward to doing clinical rotations where we got to practice the skills we were learning in the classroom. As I was about to start my first rotation working with young babies, I began having bouts of severe abdominal pain and vomiting that came on without warning and lasted for a few days. Fortunately, UNC students had their own infirmary within the hospital, making it easy for me to receive treatment for a condition they couldn't seem to diagnose. I would be hospitalized for a few days, often the only patient in that section of the hospital, where I was treated with fluids and pain medicine until I felt better. My blood tests were usually normal except that my potassium levels were often dangerously low due to all the vomiting.

When there appeared to be no obvious cause for the symptoms, I was repeatedly told that I needed to reduce my stress level. These lectures about stress reduction nearly always came after I explained that I had two young daughters and that one of them had a genetic disorder. No one offered any suggestions about how to alleviate my stress, but they seemed convinced that it was the cause of the pain and vomiting—which never made sense to me. Why did they think that my stress levels were higher now that I was in graduate school instead of teaching people how to fly all day long. Then one day a nurse practitioner I had seen before came into my room as she was getting ready to leave for the day and said offhandedly, "I know it's probably unfair to lecture you about sunbathing while you are sick, but you really should stay out of the sun." I looked at her in disbelief.

"Sunbathing," I said. "Just when do you think I have time to sunbathe?"

"Well, you look very tanned," she explained, and I realized that just like when Ashley was born, I was jaundiced again. I was rolled down the hall on a gurney for an ultrasound. A doctor appeared and said, "Well, your gallbladder looks fine." *Oh no,* I thought. *Here we go again with all the reasons why I can't be jaundiced.* It took a while for me to convince him that my gallbladder had been removed, and another ultrasound to determine that what they thought was my gallbladder was my enlarged common bile duct. This is how the gallbladder sends bile for the digestion of fats and proteins to my intestines. I was sent for an endoscopy, a procedure where under sedation a doctor can use a long tube and a camera to see into the esophagus and stomach. They were able to pry open my bile duct, which he said was like, "chiseling through concrete." The procedure, which normally took less than an hour, took four hours. As the doctor was telling me this, he started to laugh. Then he asked me if I remembered anything from the procedure. When I told him that I didn't remember a thing, he said, "That's a relief. You woke up twice and yelled, 'Get those freaking things out of my mouth!'"

Unfortunately, that was not the last of my gastrointestinal issues, and two more times I ended up needing fluids through an intravenous line because of all the vomiting. One of those times was the day before I was supposed to present our research group's final thesis. My co-authors on the paper were counting on me to deliver and defend the culmination of a year's worth of research and writing, and I was determined to see it through. After another night at the infirmary, where I received several more bags of fluids, I managed to make the presentation the next morning. No one was more excited than my four partners on the project, who had all worked diligently on the report but didn't like public speaking.

It was a relief to be finishing graduate school, but there was one more obstacle in my path to graduation. During the final week of classes, when I was struggling to keep food down, Ashley was resting next to me when I noticed that she was scratching her scalp furiously. When I investigated further what I saw was more nauseating than the smell of the bone saw we used in gross anatomy. Her thick hair was infested with head lice. I had never seen or experienced this before, but I quickly realized that she had shared her affliction with her sister and me. And then the thought occurred to me that all week long my classmates and I had been practicing our newfound therapy skills on the treatment tables in our lab area. These tables had been covered with sheets and pillowcases and there was much moving around among tables—the perfect setup for distributing the pesky critters. Even though I knew that head lice were a common problem and that they favored squeaky clean hair like Ashley's, I was still mortified at the prospect that I had potentially allowed the bugs to infiltrate the hair of my classmates. I went to the professor who was overseeing the lab and confessed my situation. He told me not to worry, but it was clear who the most likely culprit was when the memo went out to students telling them to be on the look for head lice. Once again, my generous classmates took it in stride, although at graduation I noticed that all the guys had short haircuts like they had just joined the military, and most of the women had their hair tied into buns that were secured protectively under their caps. I took some consolation in how spiffy we all looked for the ceremony, even as I tried not to vomit as I waited for my turn to walk across the stage.

How Not to Fly an Airbus

I had spent two years learning about how the human body works to become a physical therapist, but ironically my next job would involve flying a first of its kind jet that was known for taking over for the flawed humans who fly it. I had several more episodes of severe pain and vomiting like I had in graduate school, but when more emergency room doctors told me there was nothing wrong with me except stress, I was medically cleared to fly again. I knew something wasn't right, but I felt powerless to get anyone to investigate further. I still had to pass the board exam to work as a physical therapist, so while I studied, I applied for a job as a simulator instructor on the Airbus A320. Much of the training for airline pilots is done in extremely realistic flight simulators. In fact, these simulators can so authentically replicate the experience of flying a particular jet that it's not uncommon that the first time a pilot flies the actual airplane is when they have a full load of passengers on board. I always thought that would make an interesting PA announcement: *Welcome aboard. I'm excited to have you with us as I finally get to fly the real airplane for the first time instead of just the simulator. Sit back, relax, and enjoy your flight.*

This job had many advantages for me at this stage of my life. It came with a full-time salary, benefits, and a twenty-hour work week. Since many of the training sessions happened at night, I envisioned being able to spend time with my daughters during the day and working part-time as a pediatric physical therapist as well. Despite the realism of the simulators, I missed being in the air and traveling to new places. Still, I knew without a support system of people at home, both Ashley and Christina needed me in one place and being a simulator instructor provided that.

Christina had already demonstrated that she understood how compelling her sister's needs were and had taken it upon herself to minimize her demands on me. This unhealthy habit became clear at one appointment when Ashley's ears were being checked for an ear infection. While the pediatrician was using the otoscope to peer into Ashley's ear canals, Christina was bouncing around the office and playing (with permission) with the doctor's stethoscope. Suddenly she stopped playing and announced to the doctor that her ears hurt too, which was a surprise to me. The doctor, also a family friend, exchanged a knowing look with me as she said, "OK, Christina, I will look at your ears too." We both were certain that this was just an innocent ploy for attention, right up to when the doctor looked in her ears and exclaimed, "Oh, my, Christina's ears look worse than Ashley's." Christina was only four at the time.

Even though I tried to make sure that Christina knew her needs were just as important as Ashley's needs were, it was hard to compete with the rushed trips to the emergency room as Ashley spiked fevers as high as one-hundred-five degrees and turned blue from rapidly falling oxygen levels. I would like to be able to say that my efforts paid off, but when Christina graduated from high school, I suddenly realized that I had not once been asked to sign a permission slip for her even though Ashley seemed to be bringing home an endless supply of them. When I asked Christina about this, she sheepishly admitted that she had asked a friend to practice forging my signature for the past four years so that she wouldn't need to bother me. He had successfully signed off on multiple class trips and on two occasions he had circumvented my approval so she could watch an "R" rated film in class. This not only made me feel like the worst mother for not realizing it sooner, but it showed Christina's commitment to the forgery that she had her friend practice my signature. I'm not sure why she thought anyone would know the difference, but my oldest daughter has never been known for doing anything halfway.

I thought that it would be easy for me to get the job as a simulator instructor on the Airbus A320. I was already working for this airline teaching pilot ground school, and I knew the qualifications of the applicants who had been hired before me. I had more flight experience than the last six instructors who were hired, and I had recently received a performance bonus for my teaching skills and for writing training articles for the pilots. The one thing that caused me a bit of concern was that there were no full-time simulator instructors who were female, and the last two women who had been hired to fly the Airbus were terminated when they failed to make it through the rigorous training. To become an instructor, you had to get a special certification to fly the Airbus called a type rating. This involved passing numerous written tests, an eight-hour oral exam, and completing a checkride.

Despite the fact this was the year 2001, and many things had changed since I had started flying in 1974, the field of aviation remained remarkably unchanged in its gender diversity. Equally disturbing was the fact that I suspected the attitude of the captain doing the hiring was shockingly like the few pilots in my past who felt that if the last woman they hired had struggled through training it predicted the flying skills of all female pilots. My suspicions were confirmed when the hiring manager called me into his office which was just down the hall from mine. This Airbus captain had white hair and a perpetual scowl on his face. We crossed paths in the hallway multiple times a day and he never acknowledged my polite greetings or even made eye contact with me. Despite my suspicions that gender played a role in his hiring decisions, I was still shocked at his willingness to unabashedly reveal his true thoughts on the matter of women flying the Airbus.

"You must be tough to fly the Airbus. Learning how to fly it has made grown men cry," he explained, as if that was all he needed to say on the subject. Did he really think I was going to just walk away?

"Maybe you should hire some women then," I said. That did not get me the job.

Fortunately, his tenure in this position was short-lived, and when another pilot was put in the position I applied once again. This time I was hired after a real interview. Although I had experience flying an airplane which had computer screens like the Airbus in place of the traditional flight instruments which were still being used in Boeing airplanes at the time, I still hadn't flown anything faster than a Cessna-172 for about eight years. The director of flight training told me that I might want to refresh my flying skills by using a flight simulator or renting an airplane, but then he thought better of it. He said, "The Airbus is unlike any other airplane, so it probably won't help." It was an ominous warning, but accurate. Nothing I could have flown would have prepared me for the unique characteristics of the Airbus.

The hardest part about flying an Airbus is acknowledging the ways that the Airbus doesn't need you. It was the first fly-by-wire jet, where mechanical connections between the control surfaces and the pilot controls that move them were replaced with switches that send a signal to hydraulically move the control surface. It saved an enormous amount of weight and allowed the Airbus to be more fuel efficient, along with other benefits. The Airbus was also designed to keep the pilot out of trouble with flight protection systems that prevent a pilot from over speeding it, rolling into a steep bank, or stalling it. Whereas other jets, like the Boeing 737 and other Boeing jets, warn pilots of impending doom but ultimately let the pilots do what they want, the Airbus warns pilots if they are flying too slowly or raising the nose too high and then takes corrective action if the pilots fail to respond. This was a new way of thinking about the role of the pilot that was not always welcomed. If you have a personality that lends itself to being a bit of a control freak, then the Airbus is not the airplane for you. If it sounds like you might feel like you are a passenger instead of a pilot at times, especially until you understand how the Airbus systems work, you would be right.

It's also not surprising that one of the places where pilots run into trouble flying the Airbus is when they decide to do things their own way ultimately and end up interfering with the many automated processes. Since I worked in flight crew training, I got to hear a lot of stories about pilot-induced problems brought on by crews not wanting to be outsmarted by their own airplane. It never ended well. Take the crew that decided that even though the fuel system automatically burns fuel from the tanks in the wings and the center tank in the fuselage in a prescribed way, they were going to do it their own way. The problem is that by doing it themselves in a different manner, they ended up pumping fuel into a tank that was already full. What happened next was the flight attendant called to explain that an attentive passenger sitting over the wing said it looked like fuel was being pumped overboard from the wing. Although the crew knew right away how to undo the problem they created, how were they going to explain it? They could blame it on a mechanical problem, but then they would need to return to the airport. Or they could say that they fixed the issue, but undoubtedly some passengers would still be worried. Ultimately, they had no real choice but to return to the airport. It was best for everyone if the pilots came to the point where they trusted the automated systems to run things while they monitored it—and then they just had to let it go.

The Airbus has some other features (along with other sophisticated jets) that can challenge even an experienced pilot. To make it easy to abort a landing, a pilot can simply push a button on the thrust levers which will add full thrust, also known as takeoff/go around or TOGA. The problem is that now you will find yourself climbing and accelerating very quickly. Since most of the time you take off with less than full power, TOGA power is quite a shock. It might even be cool if you were trying to get somewhere in a hurry, but since you are trying to land, you now need to slow down and stop climbing and that is not as easy as just pressing a button. While you are trying to recall how to undo this it can feel like what I imagine my eighty-year-old mother experienced when she went snow tubing and forgot she needed to slow down by using her feet which were tucked tightly under her butt. She went zipping down the hill and over the barrier into the parking lot. Flying the Airbus can feel a lot like that.

The training program was a challenge for me, and not just because this was my first jet, or because I had flown smaller "puddle jumpers" for a long time. One of my most memorable training sessions was with a retired captain in his eighties who took one look at me in the briefing room and said, "I just have to tell you about my first experience flying with a woman." My first officer flashed me a look that said *I'm sorry in advance if this is bad, but we probably should let him say his piece.* I took a deep breath and listened. The instructor then launched into this story of how as a captain he was not pleased the first time he was assigned to fly with a female first officer. He shared how he had told his first officer his long list of why women shouldn't be pilots. I will not repeat the list of dumb reasons here, but he described how his first officer sat there patiently waiting for him to end his tirade and then she said, "Are you done now because I really want to get this motherfucker off the ground." He relayed this story with obvious admiration for this woman who had showed him what an idiot he was being. So even though the story ended well, and he turned out to be one of the best instructors, it seemed like I was always waiting for the next person to share their history with women in aviation and make judgments of me based on that.

Besides the comments I had already heard about the Airbus being too tough for a woman to fly, there was also a group of pilots who didn't like the experience level of some of the simulator instructors who were being hired. These pilots wanted all simulator instructors to be pilots who had retired from the airline. They were rightfully upset that many of the simulator instructors hired before me had no airline experience at all. It was difficult to see how someone who had never flown for an airline could create realistic training scenarios in the simulators. Even though I had airline experience, many pilots just assumed that I did not. I felt like I had to prove myself for this reason and because I was also just thirty-eight years old, which made me the youngest simulator instructor by a couple of *decades*.

I understood the frustrations of some pilots who flew with simulator instructors who knew far less than they did about how to fly an Airbus. I had experienced this myself during my training when I was scheduled one night to train with a former pilot ground instructor who had been hired right before me as a simulator instructor. While he was a colleague who I got along well with, I also knew that he had no airline experience and that he had failed his checkride in the Airbus three times before finally passing. He had also failed the oral exam and had to retake it. I thought that there was no excuse for someone who was going to teach in the Airbus to fail their oral exam. How did they expect to teach in it if they didn't know everything there was to know about it? Now he was suddenly teaching me, but he still failed to understand the hydraulic systems on the Airbus.

During one of our sessions, he failed two of the three hydraulic systems that controlled the landing gear and the flaps. The problem was that the gear and the flaps were already down, and he also failed one of my engines. Not only was this an implausible situation to have all those failures at once, but after I set up for an emergency landing and was close to landing, he directed me to abort the landing by going around. I knew the Airbus was not going to climb on one engine with all that drag from having full flaps down and the gear down and there was no way for me to get the gear and flaps back up, so I refused to go around thinking he was somehow testing me. Apparently, it was not a test. He insisted that it was possible and that I do it anyway, which prompted me to remind him about the emergency button we could push in the event of an impending crash of the simulator. The simulator was a couple of stories off the ground and when it crashed it was possible to not only get tossed around badly but it could do damage to the equipment—hence the button that froze everything and lowered the simulator slowly and safely back to ground level. The one problem with using it was that the simulator would have to be restarted by the technicians, and everyone involved would naturally assume that whoever was the student at the time must have really screwed up. I didn't want anyone to think that I was the one who crashed it, especially when I already felt like all eyes were on me. Sure enough, as I added power it was clear that we were going to crash. We both went to hit the "stop" button, but I made him tell everyone that he had asked me to do something that was impossible. He might have gotten three shots at his checkride, but I had no illusions that I was going to be given so many chances.

Given everything, I was already dubious when my checkride came around that I would be able to pass it. I knew I *could* pass it, but I figured passing it depended less on me and more on whether the pilot who was testing me, called a check pilot, thought that I deserved to be a simulator instructor or not. I just wanted a fair ride by the book. I suspected I was in trouble when I showed up for the checkride and found myself facing a check pilot whose disdain for me was as evident as the cowboy hat on his head. I knew of him by reputation only. He was a former chief pilot for our airline who seemed like a poor fit for a management position given his abrasive personality. He seemed to take his cues on how to act from another age where machismo was expected of men and silent adoration of those same men was expected of the female folk. He owned a massive cattle ranch in Durango and had seemingly few admirers at the airline except for himself.

I suspected my situation was going to be further complicated by the fact that the pilot that had been called in to take on the duties as my first officer was more nervous than I was. They didn't put me with my usual simulator partner for the checkride, which would have been preferable since we knew each other's habits, but instead called this first officer on short notice and gave him the unwanted assignment. This was not a predicament that any first officer wanted to be in. Even though technically he wasn't being tested, there was still a chance he could be given a poor evaluation by this check pilot. He had been a first officer for only nine months, so he was still on probation. This meant that he could be more easily terminated, and I suspect that he was keenly aware of the jeopardy he was in.

I knew this first officer and liked him, as I had been his

instructor in ground school when he first came to the airline. He was also the opposite of the check pilot in his demeanor. His exuberant greeting to me clearly annoyed the check pilot who made an obscene gesture behind his back indicating that the check airman thought this first officer was gay and that he didn't approve. I'm sad to say that I was not shocked, as homophobia was not uncommon among many pilots I had flown with, even some of those who championed my presence on the flight deck as a female.

The check pilot was all business as I was tested on the many calamities that can befall a flight such as engine fires, engine failures, and multiple approaches in bad weather to different airports. All seemed to be going fine until we had to divert to a different airport from the destination we had programmed into the computer. Making things happen using the computerized systems on the Airbus is often easier than making them unhappen, and this is true for when you are rerouted to a new airport. You must first find the correct screen in the computer's flight management system to set up the new route. There are many ways to do this, none of them are intuitive, and you can't google it. My first officer hadn't diverted to another airport since his initial training nine months before, and so he naturally forgot how to do it. I became aware of this when I looked over at him after hearing frantic typing on the computer's keys and saw rivulets of sweat running down his panicked face. The solution was straightforward—I needed to let him fly so that I could program the computer. There is a specific way to do this because it's crucial that both pilots know who is flying the airplane at any given moment—keeping in mind it might not be obvious because the autopilot is often on. I told my first officer that he should take over flying the airplane by saying, "your airplane" and waiting for him to say, "my airplane." And then I said again, "your airplane," per the protocol. My first officer looked relieved as I got us set up to fly to the new destination, and I was proud of myself for not getting unnerved by this glitch.

I was starting to feel like maybe I would pass this test after all because we were close to the end, and I knew I had flown everything according to the standards. We only had one thing left to do and it was called an autoland. It is what it sounds like—the airplane flies itself all the way to the ground and lands itself. I reasoned there was little chance of failing the test doing an autoland since the pilot's job is mainly to watch it happen. As easy as it is to do, it can be stressful, especially the first time you do it. It feels like you are waiting for the nose to crash into the runway, which you are, and at the last moment the airplane will nose up by itself for the landing flare. The pilot must sit there, watching intently, but not let their anxiety get the best of them. It's a leap of faith to trust that the system will work, but you also must let it do its job.

As the Airbus landed itself, I felt relieved that the checkride was over, but not the satisfaction of knowing that I had passed. I suspected this check pilot was going to find something to justify failing me. He quickly got out of the simulator without a word, leaving my first officer and me gathering up our flight bags. My first officer apologized profusely for his stumble with the flight management system, but I assured him it was not a problem. Then he congratulated me, extending his hand. Without thinking, I said no congratulations were in order, and he seemed dumbfounded.

"But you did everything to the standards. How can he fail you?" he asked, truly surprised and disappointed for me.

"I don't know what excuse he will use to fail me, but he will. I am sure of it," I said solemnly. What happened next still upsets me to this day because I had never failed a checkride and I knew I met the standards for this one. This wasn't about how I performed; it was about his ego and showing his displeasure about the pilots (and perhaps especially this female one) that were being hired as simulator instructors.

Sure enough, as I entered the office the check pilot was typing out the paperwork for a checkride failure known as a "pink slip." (It used to be on pink paper.) He had to note the specific items I had failed, and he was so cocky that he said I failed on the autoland procedure. I was baffled and humiliated. It would have been easier to handle if he said that I hadn't handled something difficult like the hydraulic failure, or the rapid depressurization that required us to do an emergency descent and put the full-face mask on while flying, but instead he said I didn't properly watch the Airbus land itself.

I decided that I had nothing to lose, so I asked him to explain his reasoning. He said that my first officer had forgotten to push the button for autoland on the right side of the panel (there was one on each side), and although the airplane would autoland (and did) just fine with one button engaged, it was company policy to push both buttons for redundancy. I had not seen the first officer's error even though I had properly announced that both buttons needed to be engaged. I must have been the only person in history who had to take my checkride over for something that involved *not* flying the airplane. It was not my first officer's fault, and I am glad that he wasn't there to hear why they were failing me, but it was dubious that my only mistake was not catching a button push that didn't affect how the airplane flew or functioned. To me it was clearly a "in your face" move.

I desperately hoped that I would get to do the checkride over with a different check pilot. I had to wait a few days to find out, and in that time, I heard from nearly everyone who had trained me on the Airbus—instructors who would be my colleagues if I ever passed my checkride—that they were livid about what had happened. They confirmed my suspicions that no matter how well I did, my fate with this check pilot was determined before I had buckled into the left seat.

A few days later I was rescheduled for the test and was thrilled to find out that I would be tested by a different check pilot. He was dumbfounded when he saw what had happened on the previous test. I took that as a good sign. He could have tested me on everything again, but he decided that he would test me only on that one item. I took off, put the autopilot on, watched as it did an approach, and then watched it autoland. It was a quick test, and a monkey could have done it. I was relieved to finally have this ordeal over with, but I didn't feel like celebrating. I was so disappointed that I had failed a checkride.

I didn't know it then, but it would be the last checkride that I would ever take. It was August of 2001, and in less than two months the airline would terminate half of the simulator instructors because of the terrorist attacks. I was called on my day off at ten in the morning to report at noon to turn in my badge. When I told human resources that my daughter was sick, and I couldn't come in until the next day when I was scheduled to work, they got angry and told me I had to come right away. With all the tragedies that had just unfolded, I couldn't understand why they were being so petty. I finally told them if they were so anxious to fire me that it couldn't wait a day then they could come to my house and get my freaking badge. It was a tough time for everyone, and my airline was reeling from the realization that our own pilots and flight attendants were at risk to terrorists while just doing their jobs. Yet one of the first actions they took was to terminate instructors like me who had just completed training even though it would cost far more to train new instructors when flying activity resumed. It never made sense, but not much made sense for anyone who loved to fly and were angered by the thought that the terrorists had used airplanes as weapons of destruction. I later found out that one of my flight students was the son of the first officer on one of the jets that hit the tower that day. He is now a pilot for the same airline as his father.

I ended up returning to teaching at the New Hampshire college where I previously worked. This meant that on January 15, 2009, when Sully and his crew ditched their Airbus in the Hudson, I was inundated with phone calls from various media outlets requesting interviews on how to ditch an Airbus. I was in the middle of doing a phone interview with *Popular Mechanics* on another aviation subject when the news of the ditching broke, so they got my first comments on the situation as it was unfolding. I was careful not to jump to conclusions although it was clear what had happened here.

The one comment I regretted making was that it wasn't so far-fetched that an Airbus would float because it was designed with a ditching switch just for that purpose. This switch closes several openings to the outside air for things like the pressurization system and for cooling the radios. Flipping that switch in the event of a ditching makes the Airbus more airtight. I even said during an early interview that it was likely the crew didn't flip this switch given how little time they had, and that ditching was not normally practiced during training. I immediately regretted mentioning it at all because the journalist on the other end of the line was incredulous that they might have missed the one switch that was specifically meant to be used when ditching. I knew they were doing everything they could to try to get an engine restarted, and in the three minutes or so they glided they had no time to get through the ditching checklist. All the checklists are designed as if you have time to do them and they didn't have that. It seemed like a few of the fifteen journalists I talked to that day wanted something they could catch them on and I didn't understand that mentality.

One of the news outlets that contacted me was my local television station, and I did a live phone interview where I emphasized how many tasks the pilots and flight attendants had to complete in a short period of time. This resulted in them asking me to do a recreation of the sights and sounds in the cockpit during an emergency such as this. We used the college's jet training device to show them a takeoff over the same route with all the warnings that would be going off. I narrated while two pilots demonstrated what would have been happening in the cockpit. The simulation was taped for a segment to be shown later that evening on the local evening news. Since the video had to be edited before airing, I tuned in that night to see how the final product had turned out. I had done newspaper and radio interviews before, but this was my first television interview.

As I waited for my segment to air, there was a story about a man near my hometown who was arrested and charged with multiple counts of cruelty to animals. As I watched this heartbreaking story where emaciated horses and dogs were shown being rescued, I realized the man in handcuffs with the scraggly beard was a familiar face from my past. He was the biology teacher that had kept me after school in that closet so many years ago. Apparently, his neighbors had tipped off the police that he was abusing and neglecting animals. I felt a kinship with those animals. Fortunately, someone had intervened on their behalf. As I watched myself on television for the first time, I thought about how fitting it was that I was being interviewed about flying, the thing that helped me overcome the trauma he caused, while my abuser was being arrested. It made me feel like I often did at the end of a four-day trip, when I touched down at my home airport, my latest journey complete.

Grounded

When you are a pilot, every new physical symptom you develop can put you in a state of high anxiety. That's not because you necessarily fear for your life, but because you fear that whatever "it" is will keep you from flying. There is a constant struggle between the part of you that wants to see every specialist who might be able to diagnose this new thing that is happening to you, and the part that knows you will have to tell the FAA about all those appointments. You pray that any new ache or bump is something easy to diagnose and fix. It really needs to be horses, not zebras, because the FAA doesn't like zebras. It's not that you want to have an inflamed appendix, but you know they can remove it and then it's over. The folks at the FAA will be satisfied that the medical problem has been resolved and you can get back to flying.

That is what was going through my mind as I lay writhing on the floor at three on the morning of January 6, 2010. The fact that I can recall the exact date reveals a lot about how what happened on this day changed my life. I had been woken up by stabbing pain in my upper abdomen, nausea, vomiting, and a fever. The pain was the most severe that I had ever felt. Keep in mind that I had given birth to one daughter without so much as a whimper or a Tylenol, and to a second daughter where the contractions were so strong for over twenty hours that my obstetrician finally asked me to agree to an epidural because he couldn't watch me suffer any longer. This pain was worse. This was the kind of pain where you are so desperate to make it go away that dying seems like a reasonable alternative to enduring the agony for one more minute.

Typically, I would have either been home alone, or with Ashley who was in no position to help me. Because of Ashley's rare genetic condition, at this time she was much like a six-year-old in the body of a small and unsteady teenager. Her usual response to any ailment I have has always been to decide that she, too, has the same affliction. It's like she thinks we are still physically connected, like the umbilical cord was never cut. Fortunately for both of us, Christina was home on winter break from her first semester of college. I crawled into her room on the other side of our apartment, and she immediately made an amateur diagnosis of appendicitis. This was Christinia's "go to" diagnosis ever since she endured a burst appendix when she was nine. I thought she might be right. I also thought perhaps the culprit was some French fries I ate earlier in the day, but since Christina had eaten more of them than me and wasn't sick, I thought that was unlikely. Christina sat up with me, wiping my forehead with a cool cloth, as I barfed into the pot I used for boiling spaghetti.

As I shivered and barfed, I realized that this pain, although sharper in its intensity, was familiar to me. It had been nearly a decade since graduate school when doctors had used what I imagined looked like a Roto-Rooter-like device to unclog my bile duct. This pain felt like that, but more intense. By sunrise, things had calmed down and I hoped that maybe it was just the French fries. Christina and I were both relieved because she was returning to South Carolina in a few days to resume her classes, and I would no longer have her help caring for Ashley or me. Later that evening, the whole thing started again, leaving me in a fetal position on my bathroom floor.

I soon became a regular at the emergency room as I returned repeatedly with bouts of severe pain, fever, and vomiting that happened with no warning. Unlike when I was in Chapel Hill, where I could go to the school infirmary and be treated with dignity and respect, at my local emergency room back in New Hampshire I was treated like a criminal and not a patient. The opioid epidemic had struck New Hampshire particularly hard, and the response to that was to treat everyone who arrived at the emergency room complaining of pain as drug seeking unless they had an obvious reason for their pain. Even worse, if you were suspected of abusing drugs, the response was not to help you through medical intervention, but to treat you with contempt. Suddenly I was no longer just undiagnosed, I was suspected of not being in pain at all. And if they didn't believe I was in pain, then there was no reason for them to figure out what was wrong with me.

The shift in the demeanor of the nurses was dramatic once they became convinced that I was drug seeking. One nurse, who had left to get me one of those heated blankets, returned to my room with the normal blood test results but no warm blanket. She even removed the thin sheet I was shivering under, shoving the discharge papers into my hands. Another nurse who worked at a pain management clinic told me in the waiting room, in front of all the staff and other patients, that I wasn't in pain at all. The fact that I already was prescribed opioids for the unrelenting pain by my primary care doctor and had been sent to the clinic for alternative pain treatments, did nothing to dissuade her. I didn't want more painkillers; I wanted pain management without more drugs. That was the purpose of the clinic after all—it was even in their name. I felt like she was trying to make an example of me in front of all the other patients in the room.

It would have been easier if my blood tests had been abnormal, but not every ailment shows up in a blood test or shows up every time. When I kept returning to the same emergency room, always with the same symptoms, you might have thought that someone would have ordered more tests. Why would I keep going back to try to scam the same people out of painkillers? It didn't even make any sense. And even after my own doctor prescribed some painkillers, I still ended up at the emergency room when I couldn't keep the pills or anything else in my stomach. If my own doctor, the one who knew me the best, believed I was in pain, then why were the emergency room staff so quick to judge me?

On one particularly distressing night I was barely able to walk out the door of the emergency room after I was discharged with another lecture about my supposed drug abuse. The two security guards at the front desk tried to help me *back into the hospital* because I could barely walk, and they couldn't believe I was being sent home. Neither could I.

Grasping at anything that might help me, after a year of frequent hospitalizations for unrelenting vomiting, I was referred to a surgeon because of a cyst in my liver that had been discovered years prior to this. Normally these types of cysts are harmless, but given my persistent symptoms a specialist in gastrointestinal issues thought that maybe removing that part of my liver might help. It was a long shot, but he understood how debilitating the symptoms had become and thought it was worth investigating. Christina was still in South Carolina, although she had already taken one semester off to help me with Ashley. I wouldn't let anyone drive me the hour and a half ride to the surgeon's office because I was too embarrassed that he might find nothing wrong. I wanted to be alone in my misery if that turned out to be the case. So, I drove there myself, gripping the steering wheel with white knuckles because I had to stop taking the pain medicine long enough to drive there and back. Once I made it to the waiting room, all I could think about was how long was this going to take because I was feeling nauseous again and still had to drive myself back home.

I felt surprisingly comfortable with the surgeon the moment he came bounding into the room. Maybe it was because I could look him in the eye as he was close in height to me, or maybe it was because he was bald and confident. His white lab coat was pristine, and by the way he pounced on the keys of his laptop I surmised that he disliked typing his notes while his patient sat there waiting. He sent me to radiology to get an abdominal CT scan, telling me that I could leave when it was done and that he would get me on his schedule for the liver surgery after reviewing the scan. I was hopeful for the first time in a long time, and I felt like I was heard.

At radiology an intravenous line (IV) had to be inserted to inject some dye so they could get a clearer picture. As I slid on a board into the CT scanner, my belly was hurting so badly that when I was directed by the machine's robotic voice to "hold your breath" tears streamed down my face. I suppressed the urge to vomit. I knew something was amiss as soon as the scan was over. Instead of disconnecting the IV that had been inserted in my hand, a nurse offered me a wheelchair ride back to the surgeon's office. When I explained that I was supposed to be going home, the nurse said there was a change in plans and the surgeon wanted to see me again.

As I sat back in the surgeon's office, I was both relieved and scared. The thought that they found an abnormality on the scan was both worrisome and hopeful. I needed them to find something wrong to have any chance of a treatment, but the fact that there was an immediate reaction to the scan told me something was seriously wrong. As I sat there waiting for the surgeon, I again asked the nurse about removing the IV. It still hadn't registered that they needed to leave it in to give me medicine to dull the pain. "No, you might be needing that," she said.

The surgeon was blunt as he came bursting through the door like someone who doesn't have time to mince words in an operating room. "You have pancreatitis, and you can't go anywhere. You need to stay right here and be admitted to the hospital. You can die from this." The results of the scan were apparently so obvious that the surgeon said he showed some medical students the images of my inflamed pancreas. The images also showed that I had a collection of fluid that had leaked from my pancreas, called a pseudocyst, which is a telltale complication from having pancreatitis.

As soon as the surgeon told me the diagnosis, I rushed over to the little sink in the corner of his office to vomit. I don't know if it was a symptom of the pancreatitis or if I suddenly felt sick at the realization that just one scan could have diagnosed my unrelenting pain. How close was I to dying all those times an emergency room doctor was lecturing me about narcotics instead of finding out why they were the only thing that subdued my pain. This wasn't a complicated diagnosis if only someone had bothered to look. I was relieved for my pain to have a name, but it was starting to sink in that I wasn't going to be there when Ashley got home from school. I had no clothes with me, and two cats that needed to be fed. I had not prepared for this outcome.

Within a few minutes, a nurse settled me into one of those cushy reclining chairs, with lots of warm blankets, and injected some narcotic pain killers and anti-nausea medicine through the IV. I still vividly recall the nearly immediate relief I felt as the pain medicine dulled the stabbing pain in my abdomen. As my eyelids felt heavy and a warm feeling slowly made its way throughout my body as if I had been swaddled in a cashmere sweater, I thought about how much I wanted to live. The pain had been so relentless at times, and the verbal blows from doctors and nurses who were supposed to be helping me so spirit-crushing, that many times I would have accepted death as a reasonable option rather than continuing to breathe in my broken body. I was never suicidal, but I think for everyone there is a threshold of pain, whether emotional or physical or both, that when crossed makes you indifferent to the mechanism by which it can be stopped.

The surgeon seemed concerned about how long it was going to take to get me a bed in the hospital, but I was perfectly content in his office as relief took over. I heard him emphatically talking to someone on the phone. "Get her a bed now. She's vomiting in my office," he said, not like he was angry about the violation to his clean office, but like he couldn't believe that bureaucracy was going to get in the way of someone having a bed to lie down on when they were obviously so sick. It was so unlike what happened one night when I had called an ambulance because I was too weak to stand after vomiting nearly nonstop for hours. As I crawled out to the hallway in front of my apartment door to unlock a heavy fire door for the first responders, I threw up in the hallway. When the EMTs arrived, one of them said to me, "Why would you throw up there?" He said it like I was a puppy who needed training and not a sick person. I was so tired of being treated like my illness was offensive and I was wasting everyone's time. I felt protected from that as I sat in the cushy chair.

Once I got settled into a room, I was given many facts about the pancreas. Some I remembered and some I learned over time as I dozed in and out. The pancreas was described as a finicky organ that releases enzymes to digest food and contains insulin producing cells called islets that control blood sugar. Pancreatitis is an inflammation of the pancreas for which there is no cure. As one doctor put it, "Starvation is the only real treatment." A sign went up on my hospital room door saying NPO which stands for the Latin phrase nil per os or nothing by mouth. Not even sips of water were allowed past my parched lips.

I spent the next ten days in the hospital before I was well enough to go home, but I only got a short reprieve before the pain returned. Every few weeks I ended up in the hospital with pancreatitis, often for a week at a time. I kept an overnight bag packed by the door because I got violently ill with no warning. I puked once into a garbage can during the middle of a conference call at work. I could no longer fly but I was doing research and teaching various aviation topics at a college. I think I was one of their favorite professors because I had to cancel class so many times to go to the hospital. The surgeon and the rest of the pancreas team were not sure why I kept getting sick with pancreatitis, but they had said over time that they may be some surgical options if I continued being sick. I was becoming malnourished from all the vomiting, and I developed twelve cavities in my previously perfect teeth. I broke the heel bones in both of my feet at different times just from walking because I was so deficient in calcium.

After it became clear that I was not getting better, the same surgeon who had originally diagnosed my pancreatitis decided it was time to attempt to repair my pancreas in March of 2012. We knew there was no guarantee, but I was sick enough that it was worth trying to fix the problem. By this time the doctors felt that my issue was related to a birth defect with my pancreas that was affecting its ability to release the enzymes it made. This was keeping it inflamed all the time. I woke up from the surgery feeling well and recovered to the point where I was not needing any pain medicine within six weeks. I was overjoyed, but it wouldn't last.

During one of my many hospitalizations for pancreatitis the surgeon sent in a pancreas specialist to talk to me. I remember how down I was that the original surgery had not worked and how tired I was of being sick. This doctor sat down next to my bed and talked to me like he had all the time in the world. He told me that this hospital was only one of a few in the country where they could remove my pancreas and inject the islets that make insulin into my liver. If it worked and they were able to get enough islets, then my liver would do some of the work of my pancreas. It was a complicated surgery, but it offered me the first chance at a normal life again. I agreed to do it without any hesitation.

The same surgeon who performed my previous surgery did the second surgery in December of that year. My entire pancreas was removed, and the islet cells that make insulin were extracted from my pancreas nearly two hours away at a hospital lab. Then those islet cells were transported back to me where they were injected into my liver through the portal vein. The entire procedure is called a total pancreatectomy with islet auto transplantation. The "auto" part refers to the fact that my own islet cells were used. This meant that I was not required to take the anti-rejection medication that can leave a transplant patient susceptible to infections. The only question I remember asking was about how they were going to transport the islets back to me. Airplane? Helicopter? Car? I knew all the things that can go wrong in an airplane or helicopter and I obsessed about that.

I have lots of holes in my memories of the twelve days I spent in the hospital after the transplant, both good and bad. My first inkling I was going to be all right was when the surgeon said that I looked like the "Michelin Man" because of all the swelling. I figured no one would say that to a person who was dying. The scariest moment was when I was still in the intensive care unit, and I overheard a conversation between the many doctors in charge of my care. The conversation came in brief snippets as I drifted in and out because of the painkillers, but I recall a conversation about blood counts.

"I think we should do a blood transfusion now."

My heart raced and I remember wanting to scream from my bed, *yes, just give me the blood*! It was a strange feeling being too weak to speak, never mind yell, but didn't they know I could hear them talking about me right outside my door? Then there came this in response: "That number can't be right. We should recheck it. It couldn't have dropped that much overnight."

What number? Yes, it could, I thought. You want to take more blood out of me to see if I need a blood transfusion? Don't you know how crazy that sounds?

"I think we should do the transfusion and not wait," said the voice that I wanted to keep advocating for me. I fell asleep again, fitfully, worrying if more blood was coming my way. Pilots are taught if they disagree on what action to take when faced with a serious situation, they should always err on the side of being the most conservative. This means that if a captain thinks that the weather is good enough and they have enough fuel to continue, but the first officer thinks they should divert to get fuel, then they should divert. The meaning of being conservative in this context means that you go with the safer choice. I wanted to be alert enough to explain this concept to the team of doctors, to make them understand that they should do the transfusion because it was the safest decision to make. When I woke up later, I was relieved to see that one of the bags hanging from my IV pole contained a red fluid that I assumed was blood. I silently sent a thank you to the universe to all those people who donate blood.

Christina was there nearly every time that I remember waking up. Often, she was standing by my bed, holding my hand or stroking my hair, because there was no chair in the room for her. Besides being there for me, she was also taking care of Ashley. We had both tried to prepare Ashley for what I might look like when I returned home and that I would have a feeding tube. Ashley still tended to panic if I was sick, and if I had even a single Band-Aid on my body, she would remove it frantically as if no Band-Aid meant that I was all better. We were concerned about how she would handle a tube coming out of my intestines. We were right to be worried about this.

On the twelfth day after my surgery, on Christmas Eve, I was well enough to go home. My stomach was damaged from the swelling of the adjacent pancreas, and I needed several months before my digestion returned to the point where I could eat solid food. I tried to concentrate when the nurses showed me how to do my tube feeding, but as soon as I got home, I had forgotten everything. My first attempt at tube feeding found me pumping yellow liquid all over the kitchen rug while sobbing. Fortunately, Christina figured everything out, but we had to send Ashley to a sitter because she kept trying to pull my feeding tube out. I remember sobbing that I forgot to send her stocking filled with things she loved like stickers, colored pencils, and her favorite candy. It was a horrible Christmas for us all, even though I was so glad to be back in my own bed.

I spent three months at home recovering, which involved sleeping a lot and weaning off the narcotics. The feeding tube was removed after two months, but my first attempts at eating solid food resulted in vomiting. I slowly figured out what I could eat, and how much, since my stomach was smaller and slower to digest food. By May, I was feeling well enough to fly from New Hampshire to South Carolina for Christina's graduation from college. I ate steak for the first time in years. I was so happy to be there in person and to see Christina graduate on time despite everything she had done for me. She had spent a whole summer catching dragonflies and setting up ways to study their habits in a South Carolina swamp to complete her senior thesis and make up for the time she took off from college to help me.

A common complication after an islet cell transplant is slow emptying of the stomach, and nearly ten years out this is still a persistent problem. I also developed scar tissue that was removed twice by the same surgeon who did my transplant. Although I weaned off all painkillers after the surgery, I now have chronic pain due to nerve damage. It is not unlike the phantom pain experienced by patients who lose a limb. The pain is very real, but it's a nuisance type of pain rather than a sign of some acute problem or injury—except when it isn't. Sometimes my intestines just stop working and then the pain signals a serious problem like an intestinal blockage like the type that recently took the life of Elvis Presley's daughter. Living with chronic pain is hard enough, but never knowing when the pain is sending a message of an impending medical issue adds to the anxiety associated with it. And despite all that, I feel very fortunate to have been able to have my pancreas removed and the islet cells transplanted. I sent my doctors a photo of me pushing Ashley in her wheelchair as I ran my first 5K to raise money for the Special Olympics the year after the surgery.

The biggest challenge post-surgery has been the lack of knowledge about islet cell transplants by health care professionals. Many nurses, and even some doctors, are still under the impression that a pancreas can never be entirely removed. The problem is so persistent among those of us who have had our pancreas removed that our doctors have given us what looks like a business card with a bulleted list on one side. It includes information like the fact that I don't have a pancreas and a list of doctors on the pancreas team that can answer questions. Whenever I have an episode of severe pain or vomiting that takes me to a hospital, I pull the tattered card out of my wallet to prove I don't have a pancreas. Sometimes it works, but not always. On one trip to the emergency room due to chronic vomiting, a surgeon was paged to my bedside. He explained he was there to see if he needed to do surgery on my pancreas.

"I don't have a pancreas. It was removed."

"That's not possible. You can't live without a pancreas."

"I had an islet cell transplant."

I reached for the card proving that I knew which organs I had, but with a dismissive wave of his hand he said, "You didn't have your pancreas removed."

"We're done here. You can go," I said, thinking I wouldn't trust this doctor to clip my cat's claws.

When did I become this person who, just because I'm sick and in a hospital gown, can't be trusted for an accurate accounting of my own organs? I wonder sometimes if it's no coincidence that this diminished perception of my intelligence and trustworthiness has occurred while I am no longer able to fly airplanes. Perhaps my identity was so entwined with being a pilot that I put off vibes like I no longer know anything about myself. Then something will happen that reminds me that flying has changed me in such a pervasive way that even being grounded can't take that away.

Recently, I was hospitalized for eight days due to complications from the surgeries. It was the sickest I had been since my pancreas was removed. Once again, I was incapacitated quickly and without warning—just the opposite of the mental and physical stamina necessary in a professional pilot. It was a stark reminder of why I can no longer fly. Yet when I was finally wheeled to a hospital room after spending hours in the emergency department, I immediately was comforted by the fact that I had a room on the top floor of the hospital with a window overlooking the horizon to the east. I said to the orderly, with no sarcasm intended, "I'm so happy I got a room with a view." He looked dumbfounded until he realized I was serious. He made a disparaging remark about how there wasn't much to see. Yet each morning as I watched the sun rise in that window, I imagined that I was in the cockpit of an airplane, and that has made all the difference.

Air Rage

My own career as a flight instructor started off blissfully easy—other than maybe teaching my father how to fly. Three of my first students were New Hampshire state troopers, intent on being able to eventually fly the one airplane the state owned to catch speeding drivers. As is typical of New Hampshire state troopers, all three were over six feet tall and weighed more than 200 pounds. I was recruited to fly with them because I was the only flight instructor who could fit in the cramped two-seat Cessna-150 with them.

I felt oddly empowered teaching these guys, even though walking across the ramp they sometimes scooped me up and swung me off the ground like parents swinging their toddler just because they could. It wasn't meant to be sexist or demeaning, but more like how big brothers annoy their little sisters. In the airplane however, it was all business, and they showed me the respect that was often lacking when I was on the ground. It was fun flying with them, and as with many good things, I didn't appreciate it until it was over.

One of my next students also turned out to have some history with law enforcement unbeknownst to me. Roger was a friendly, energetic freshman at the college I was teaching at who became my student at the start of the semester. He had no prior flight experience, but seemed confident that he wanted a career as a pilot. He was talkative while in my office discussing the lesson for the day, and our first lesson was uneventful. (That is always a good thing).

On our next lesson, everything was going fine until I started talking him through a new maneuver and critiquing his performance. It was like a switch had gone off, and the unassuming freshman became an angry young man. As soon as I said even the most innocuous thing, like "watch your altitude" he would stop flying and begin banging his fists on the instrument panel. Even when I reassured him his performance was typical for someone with his limited flying experience, Roger continued to have what is best described as a temper tantrum. When he repeatedly rammed his elbow into the all too flimsy-looking door handle, I decided it was time to land.

As soon as we touched down, Roger was mellow again—as if nothing unusual had happened. I wasn't sure if this was a good omen or not, but I hoped that maybe he was just nervous. I tried to reassure him that he was making adequate progress and that my comments were just part of the process of learning how to fly, and he seemed not the least bit upset when we were on the ground. I even told him that he could request a different instructor and that I would understand, but that suggestion didn't work. He said he *liked* flying with me. I was puzzled, but he seemed apologetic, and I figured I would give him another chance.

We flew on our third lesson the next day, and once again he went from Bruce Banner to the Incredible Hulk as soon as I offered any suggestions on his technique. I prided myself on having a soothing voice and calm demeanor, but nothing I did quelled his rage. Once we were back on the ground, which didn't take long since I had stayed close to the airport this time, he was once again calm and contrite. I decided to broach the subject of his Jekyll and Hyde personality to see if I could learn anything for his next instructor since I had no intentions of flying with him again.

In the most therapeutic voice I could muster I said, "I notice you get upset whenever I say anything about your flying when we are in the air. You know it's my job to talk you through how to improve your flying. I'm just trying to teach you."

I immediately regretted that I had started this conversation alone in my office at the far end of the flight training center. I had once been pushed up against the wall of my office by a student who had earned a "C" in my class and thought he deserved an "A." You would think I would have learned my lesson. And yet, Roger didn't seem upset at all, and he even told me again how much he enjoyed flying with me. I remember thinking if this was him enjoying himself then I surely didn't want to see him not having fun. Then he added, almost as an afterthought, "Yeah, I have issues with my temper. That's why I'm out on bail. I was going to tell you I might miss a few lessons for my trial."

I pondered whether I should ask more questions or pretend like I flew with students every day that needed to take a break from flying lessons to face a jury of their peers.

"I killed a man," he said, as if this explained everything. In a way it did.

I thought maybe I should say something soothing.

"Oh wow," I said. "That's a lot to handle. It must be a stressful time for you. Maybe you should take a break from flying until after the trial."

I recognize how lame this sounds as I write it, but consider that I was just twenty-three years old, fresh out of college, from a small town where the fact that "Local Twins Turn Ten" was considered newsworthy. The last murder we had in our town resulted from a dispute between feuding neighbors where the murder weapon was a bow and arrow.

I desperately hoped that Roger wouldn't see my suggestion to take a break from flying as a ruse to get out of climbing into a tiny cockpit with him.

"No, I just need a few days off," he said nonchalantly, as if he was going on spring break instead of trying to stay out of prison.

I decided right then that I was going to tell the chief flight instructor that I couldn't fly with him anymore, and that maybe no one else should either. And that I wanted a lock for my office door, and maybe a new office in another building on the far side of campus. Then as if Roger was somehow reading my mind he added, "I'll probably see you around anyway. You live in the building next to mine."

Too Close to Home

One of the most challenging parts of being an instructor is to learn how to do the more advanced lessons when the "student" is already a pilot. Complacency can be more of an issue when you know the person in the left seat already has some flying skills. This can be especially true when doing longer flights to multiple airports. These lessons can be fun because you often get to fly to interesting places, but after a long day of flying it can be easy to let your guard down. I often sought out examples of accidents with advanced students to remind myself of this risk and to teach others about it. Sometimes the circumstances surrounding an accident during an instructional flight could feel chillingly close to home.

One such accident occurred on a clear November evening when a flight instructor, her student, the student's girlfriend and his brother took off from Palm Beach International Airport. They were in a Piper Seminole, a low-wing airplane with two engines, a T-shaped tail, and a long pointy nose, that is often used for training pilots. The airplane was owned by a well-respected Florida college as part of their aviation program. For the student, who was already a commercial pilot, this flight met one of his final flight requirements for his graduation from the college's professional pilot program. The foursome had just returned from the Bahamas where the student got to experience clearing customs in a private airplane and learn what it was like to fly outside of the United States. The airplane was almost certainly at its maximum weight limit because of the two passengers—a fact that didn't cause the accident but made the Seminole climb more slowly. It was around 6 P.M. and the sun had already set as they lifted off for the short hop to their home airport. Only seconds off the ground, the left engine quit.

This accident got my attention because it was much like the lessons I conducted in a Piper Seminole for my college aviation program, except my students and I flew from New Hampshire to major airports in Canada instead of Florida to the Bahamas. Many of my students said this part of their flight training, where they got to fly into major airports alongside airliners and corporate jets that they one day hoped to fly, was the first time they felt like professional pilots. No doubt it was an equally exciting time for this student and his girlfriend who were both due to graduate in a month. As it turned out, their diplomas would have to be given to their parents posthumously.

All four occupants of the airplane had some connection to this Florida college. The student's brother was twenty-six and an alumnus who also worked for the college. The flight instructor, who was also twenty-six and an alumnus, had accumulated over two-thousand flight hours—enough to qualify her to fly for an airline. The student and his girlfriend were both twenty-one. The instructor and her student were likely tired and anxious to return to their home airport now that the fun part of the trip was over. This stop in West Palm Beach was a necessary one for them to clear customs—something they couldn't do at their home airport in Melbourne.

No doubt the two passengers in the back were ready to get out of the cramped back seat where there is little room to stretch your legs, and your head can bump the ceiling in turbulence. This last leg of the trip home was just a short hop for them, maybe twenty minutes of flying time over familiar terrain. Like a driver nearing home after navigating around an unfamiliar city, they may have been less attentive to their surroundings now that they were over their home turf. Perhaps they were hungry too, given the hour, and dehydrated from a mixture of sun and restricting fluids so that they could make it between airports without needing to pee. I know this is how I felt after completing similar flights. It's hard to know if they were rushing which can lead to mistakes, but less than ten minutes elapsed from the start of the first engine to the crash. They were barely off the runway, less than two-hundred feet in the air, when the left engine quit.

The first indication of a problem occurred within seconds after takeoff when the instructor announced to the control tower that they needed to return to the airport because of an engine failure. The fact that she made this radio call at all piqued my interest. I was surprised she felt like she had the mental capacity to talk on the radio in such a dire situation. Perhaps she felt that talking to the tower was more urgent given that they had just taken off from a busy airport, but I suspect she also felt confident about her ability to handle having one engine fail in an airplane that had two engines. Yet this is one of the dangers of flying a small twin-engine (two engine) airplane—the fallacy of thinking that the second engine is going to somehow keep you in the air. I found this kind of flight instructing to be some of the most rewarding, but also some of the most challenging to do. It requires the most preparation and planning to do well because having two engines versus one provides more options to think about.

We know the instructor was calm on the radio, with no sense of alarm in her voice, as if climbing and returning to land was a reasonable option for the heavily loaded airplane. It's easy to sit safely on the ground and say confidently that it was not an option, but this is the point. The time to decide what you can do if an engine fails on takeoff is before you get off the ground. They were already flying well below the minimum speed needed to keep the airplane safely in the air, and they had all the drag that comes with still having the landing gear down. The fact that the landing gear was still down should have reinforced how impossible it was to climb. Even if they had time to get the gear up, which they did not, this airplane was not capable of climbing on one engine given its weight and speed. They would have had to *lower* the nose to get enough airspeed to continue flying, and that meant they had no option but to go down by bringing the throttles back and landing where they could. You might as well not have the second engine because it's just making you think about options you don't have.

I say this while recognizing that it might seem insensitive, perhaps even cruel, to analyze a pilot's decision making after a fatal accident. We do this as pilots and instructors because of our desire to learn from the mistakes of others. We do it to try to save the next person, while being thankful we were not given this ultimate test of our abilities as pilots. We recognize that we weren't there, that we didn't have to feel our body tense with the sudden loss of engine noise or see the wide-eyed look on our student's face. We weren't faced with the knowledge that we are going down while looking out the window and seeing nothing but bad places to land are in front of us. It's the difference between taking a written test on how to administer CPR and being faced with a lifeless swimmer on a beach with no one around to help.

Besides the fact that the airplane wasn't going to climb, there was also the challenge of controlling the airplane because that dead engine creates a lot of drag. Because of this, the airplane was being pulled and rolled to the left as soon as the engine quit. At such a low speed, this tendency would have been even more pronounced. As the airplane's speed deteriorated rapidly, their only option to keep from rolling into the ground was to pull the throttles back and land where they could. That was the only option from the start, but the fact that they still had power from one engine can provide false hope that continuing to fly is possible. It's so tempting to give it a try, especially if what lies ahead of you on the ground are buildings with people in them, but the laws of physics will win every time.

The best way to counteract the impulse to try to climb on one engine is for pilots to calculate their climb performance using the airplane's flight manual before each takeoff and then use that information to come up with a plan. Then the pilot should say out loud what their plan is in the event of an engine failure. This is called a takeoff briefing and it's a requirement among airline pilots and highly recommended for all pilots. It's even suggested that a pilot flying alone do a takeoff briefing out loud to themselves to reinforce what actions they will take if an engine fails.

The checklist for the Seminole is explicit about the steps to be taken for an engine failure on takeoff. The checklist says that if an engine fails while the landing gear is still down, or the airspeed is below eighty-eight knots (a speed marked by a blue line on the airspeed indicator in the Seminole), the procedure is to pull back both throttles to the idle position and land on what is in front of you. The highest speed this airplane reached was around seventy-seven knots, and the gear was down, making the decision to turn around even more unfathomable. Shortly after the instructor's radio transmission about turning around, the plane rolled nose down to the left onto airport property. It was a tragic but foreseeable outcome. Three of the airplane's occupants died instantly, while the brother of the pilot in the left seat died on the way to the hospital.

As it turned out, the cause of this engine failure was obvious when investigators got a look inside the cockpit. The left fuel selector lever was in the off position meaning that no fuel was being pumped to that engine from the fuel tank in the left wing. The way this could happen was no surprise to anyone who has flown a Seminole. There is a fuel selector lever for each of the two engines that has a 3-position switch: on, off, and crossfeed. Normally both fuel selectors levers will be in the on position in flight which means that fuel for the left engine comes from the left fuel tank in the wing, and similarly for the right. If a fuel selector lever is off, then there is no fuel coming from either fuel tank to that engine. If a fuel selector lever is at crossfeed, that engine is getting fuel from the tank in the other wing. So, a left fuel selector lever at crossfeed means the left engine is receiving fuel from the tank in the right wing.

The checklist instructs the pilot to switch the two fuel selectors levers to the crossfeed position while taxiing. This allows the pilot to confirm that fuel can flow from the right tank to the left engine, or vice versa. To accomplish this, you must turn the fuel selector levers from on, *through the off position,* and then to crossfeed. These fuel selector levers are located on the floor between the two seats in the front. They are easy to reach with your hand, but somewhat hard to see from the front seat since they sit toward the back. There is an indentation between each position to help you feel what you are doing. Even though there is a reminder on the checklist to return the levers back to "on" before takeoff, it's possible to miss it, or to mistakenly leave one or both fuel selectors levers in "off" while attempting to move them through the off position and back to "on."

You might think that the engine would quit right away while they were still on the ground. Unfortunately, it's a more dangerous situation. It can take some time for the engine to run out of fuel. To understand how this can happen, imagine a garden hose where there is some water still in the hose, but there is no new water coming from the spicket because it's shut off. You will be able to get some water from the hose, but it will soon run out. In the case of the Seminole, there was enough fuel in the fuel line to get off the ground with the left engine running, but once that ran out the engine quit. As it turns out, that happened to be less than two-hundred feet above the ground—one of the worst places to have an engine failure unless you are mentally prepared to land the airplane, and you have a place to put it.

I think this accident got to me because I had seen firsthand how easy it was for a pilot to unintentionally leave the fuel selector levers in the wrong position. I was flying with a student a few years before this accident when I saw both fuel selector levers had been left in the crossfeed position after we were hundreds of feet in the air. The operating manual for the Seminole prohibits taking off with the fuel selector levers in the crossfeed position, although it doesn't specify why, and in our case the engines kept running fine. I was still uneasy about it because I knew if I missed seeing that they were in the crossfeed position, then I could have just as easily missed it if either one of them had been left in the off position. After that I made a habit of checking the fuel selector levers on every takeoff right before we pushed the throttles forward. I later was flying in the back seat observing another instructor doing training in a Seminole when I saw that one of the fuel selector levers was in the wrong position. It was almost easier to see it from the back seat than from one of the front seats. I pointed it out before we took off, but I knew how easy it was to make such a mistake.

When the investigation of this accident was completed, I read through it carefully, feeling an obligation to use it for training purposes for both my students and for the flight instructors I trained to teach in the Seminole. As I read the report a second time, I learned another detail that I had previously missed. The student's girlfriend, who was in the back of the Seminole on that fateful flight, was also a flight instructor at the same college. I knew from my experience that at some point she might have seen that the left fuel selector lever was off from the back seat. I could only hope that in her final moments she didn't see it—the cause of the engine failure—after it was too late.

Mayday

I was a twenty-three-year-old flight instructor working for a college in New Hampshire when I had to make my first emergency landing due to an engine failure. My student on that warm and hazy Friday afternoon in September was Rob. He was the kind of student you wanted to be flying with if the only engine in your airplane was about to tear itself apart.

Rob was a clean-cut twenty-one-year-old planning a career flying for the Air Force. He was already a private pilot with about two-hundred hours of flight time and the most experienced of all my students. We were flying that day in a Mooney M20J, a sleek four-seater that was one of my favorite airplanes to teach in. My students were all pursuing their commercial pilot's certificates along with their bachelor's degrees in aviation flight operations. The Mooney's speed, and the challenges of slowing it down for landings, made it a great airplane for training pilots who would one day be flying airliners and corporate jets. It also could glide well—as we were soon to find out.

On this afternoon we would have two passengers in the back. Since this was one of Rob's last training flights before he took his checkride to become a commercial pilot, I liked the idea of having a full airplane. Training flights often consisted of just the training pilot and the instructor, but it's more realistic to have passengers or cargo on board. The plane flies differently with the added weight in the back, and passengers can be distracting for the pilot—both good things for this stage of Rob's training. So, when Rob asked if his buddy, Jim, could ride along, I was all for it. Jim was hoping to fly helicopters in the Army and wanted to see what a flying lesson was like. The other passenger was Sherry, who had been bugging me for a ride in the Mooney for the past year. At the time, Sherry was a low-time private pilot who flew the more docile Cessna Skyhawk for fun. Getting to fly in the Mooney was like going from a ride in a Volvo station wagon to riding in a Jag—except with less leg room.

This Mooney, like many smaller airplanes, had two sets of flight controls and could be flown from either seat. I was in the right seat, which is typical when you are instructing, and Rob was flying from the left seat. The cockpit was uncomfortably warm, with the only cool air coming from two quarter-sized vents to the outside on each side of the cockpit. It was a bumpy ride, and it seemed like every pilot in the area had left work early to go flying. There was constant chatter over the radio as pilots talked to air traffic control. Rob had tried to request permission to fly through the area around the airport in Manchester, New Hampshire on our way back to our home airport in Nashua, but the controller was too busy to talk to us. The voices on the radio were regularly being interrupted by a loud squeal, the sound made when two radios are transmitting at the same time. We had given up trying to talk to the controller and climbed from three-thousand feet to three-thousand-five-hundred feet so we could fly over the airport without needing permission. It turned out that those extra five-hundred feet were going to come in handy.

In a bit of good luck, we were flying over terrain that was familiar to me when things started to go awry. I had flown this route as a student pilot on one of my first solo flights at the age of sixteen. Below us I could see a small group of ponds. I recalled circling over these ponds on that first solo trip while I summoned the courage to transmit my intentions to land at Manchester to the control tower. Because of this I knew we were about eight miles northeast of the airport even though I couldn't see the two intersecting runways at Manchester in the haze. We were flying southwest into the setting sun, and just like driving into the sun can be blinding, flying into the sun on a hazy day can make it hard to see anything up ahead. Because of this we could only see about four miles in front of us.

Rob couldn't see anything except for the instrument panel because he was wearing a white plastic visor called a hood that blocked his view out the windows sort of like blinders on a horse. I was having Rob practice flying using only the flight instruments since he would need to do this on his upcoming checkride. To make things more challenging, I had covered up some of the flight instruments with sticky notes. Rob was sweating, trying to hold his altitude in turbulence while bright pink pieces of paper covered the instruments that would have been most useful to him.

There were some snickers from Jim in the back as I kept giving Rob more things to do, part of my strategy to see if he could juggle multiple tasks and set priorities. I was secretly enjoying thinking of ways to challenge him without being unrealistic about what I was asking him to do. Rob had been one of my first students when I started instructing at the college. His calm demeanor, combined with his skill as a pilot and sense of humor, made flying with him enjoyable. He always took whatever challenges I dished out to him in stride, and we had flown this Mooney to places like Reagan National Airport in Washington, D.C., and Montreal-Mirabel Airport in Quebec. I was feeling a bit nostalgic since this was likely one of our last training flights together.

As I turned my attention from looking out the window for other airplanes and back to scanning the instruments, something on the far left side of the panel caught my attention. The oil pressure and temperature gauges were two small round dials, each with a needle that should have been pointing somewhere near the middle of a clearly marked green arc. Instead, both needles were pointing to zero, much like what you would see if a gas gauge was on empty. This meant that the gauges were not registering any oil pressure or temperature, which could only mean two things—either both gauges had failed at the same time, an unlikely possibility, or there was no oil left in the engine to measure. Although the engine was still running smoothly, it was like seeing lightning and waiting for the inevitable rumble of thunder. I knew things were not going to remain as they were for long. At that instant I was the only one in the airplane who knew it.

I took a few moments to ponder our options. Just like in a car, oil plays a vital role in the lubrication of an airplane engine's many moving parts. Without oil, the engine would tear itself apart, leaving us able to fly only as far as we could glide. There was a risk that as the unlubricated parts of the engine scraped against each other something might break loose from the intense vibrations. This could make the airplane unflyable. If we shut down the engine as a precaution against this, I wasn't sure that we could glide to the airport. Rob had still not noticed the abnormal readings even though these two gauges were directly in front of him while I had to strain to see them from the right side of the cockpit. Yet I also knew that when something is nearly always pointing where it should be, you tend to not notice it after a while.

"Rob, look at this," I said quietly while pointing at the gauges, hoping not to alarm our passengers in the back. For a moment I suspect he was hoping that I had somehow "failed" those instruments too and that this was just part of the lesson. I often popped the circuit breakers to instruments like the fuel gauges to see if students noticed they were on empty, but as Rob quickly turned to look at me, the white hood obstructing his view still on his head, I could see in his eyes that he knew this was the real deal.

Rob threw the hood in the back as I ripped the sticky notes off the flight instruments. I looked at the ground below us to see if there was any place we could make an emergency landing if the engine failed before we could make it to an airport. I saw the only open area was a small pond surrounded by trees. The highways were full of Friday afternoon traffic, and every field I could see had either a tree in the middle of it or was much too small. I figured the one thing I could do right now that might help us was to let air traffic control know that we had an emergency so they could direct us toward the airport—or at least know where we went down.

Like most airplanes, we had a transponder which could be used to alert air traffic control that we had an emergency and help to identify us on the controller's radar screen. I could use the four black knobs on the front of the device to select the numbers 7-7-0-0. This code, known as a squawk code, is the one used for an emergency. It would make the otherwise inconspicuous dot that represented our airplane on the controller's radar screen into an immediately noticeable symbol of an emergency. I could have also used the radio to transmit our emergency using the words "mayday" three times, but I wanted to be focused on what was about to happen rather than trying to get a word in on the busy frequency. As it turned out, I had only managed to turn the first two round knobs to "7" before the familiar purr of the engine decreased suddenly.

It may sound strange, but the first thing Rob and I did was look at each other's hands to see if the other had pulled back the power using the one throttle. It was like our brains didn't want to accept that this airplane that had safely kept us airborne and responded so predictably to our inputs had suddenly gone rogue.

This was nothing like the soothing silence I was used to when I intentionally turned off the engine in the motorized gliders I flew. There was a loud bang and a sudden deafening noise not unlike the sound of an overloaded washing machine. Gray smoke poured into the cockpit, and the flight controls and instrument panel were shaking so badly that we were unable to see our altitude, airspeed, or what radio frequency we were on. It smelled like driving behind an old car with an oil leak mixed with the scent of a hot iron.

I had taken the flight controls from Rob when he had thrown off the hood, and now I turned the airplane in what I hoped was the right direction to put us on a perpendicular path to the longest of Manchester's two runways. It was a path that would also keep us away from the most populated city in New Hampshire. I could hear the controller telling other airplanes on the frequency that there was an airplane with an emergency as he started to clear planes out of our way. Soon he was calling us, trying to find out what was going on and how he could help us. "How many souls on board and how much fuel do you have?" he asked, standard questions for when an airplane has an emergency.

I didn't respond right away to him. The controller called us several times and there was an unspoken understanding between us: I knew he had to ask those questions, and he understood that I was too busy to answer him. I remember telling the controller that our engine had quit, and we needed help finding the airport. As soon as I transmitted our plight, the nonstop chatter on the radio became eerily quiet—as if everyone was waiting to hear what would come next.

Rob was already going through the checklist for shutting down the engine as I glided us toward an airport I still couldn't see through the hazy sky. Because Rob was an experienced pilot, we were working as a team. While I continued to look for the airport,

Rob pulled out the red knob next to the throttle which shut off fuel going to the engine. The noise of the engine shaking itself apart was drowning out everything except the sound of Sherry yelling from the back seat about the smoke that was pouring into the cockpit. I wish I could say that I was sympathetic to how scary it must have been to be sitting helpless in the back, but I was focused on trying to communicate with Rob and locating the airport. I could hear Jim calmly reassuring her. When that didn't work, I yelled, "Sherry shut up!" I didn't realize until later how close we had come to those being the last words I ever spoke to my twin sister.

With the fuel now shut off to the engine, the propeller slowly came to a stop. It became blissfully quiet except for the hushed sound of air moving over the wings. If I had closed my eyes, I might have convinced myself that Rob and I were doing a lesson in one of the gliders the college owned. It was not unnerving to see the propeller come to a stop; it was only odd that it was happening in a Mooney. I was glad I spent about one-hundred hours flying and teaching in gliders over the past year.

With the noise gone, I could now hear the urgent voice of a controller saying, "Twelve o'clock, twelve o' clock." His tone got more emphatic with each transmission. In my narrowly focused state of mind, I misinterpreted what the controller was saying. I was so used to air traffic control pointing out other airplanes using the hands of a clock as a reference (twelve o'clock is an airplane directly in front of you, while three o'clock indicates an airplane is off your right wing, and so on) that I recall thinking with some annoyance: *why is he pointing out traffic to me now?* It was only after I saw the airport straight ahead of us that I realized my mistake. The tension in my arms and legs dissipated because I now knew that we could glide to the runway.

Now that Rob had completed the emergency checklists, I

asked him if he wanted to take over flying the airplane again. This may seem like an unusual choice given that I had more flight experience, but as an instructor it made sense in many ways to let Rob take over flying. In fact, if Rob had not had his ability to see outside blocked by the hood when the engine failed, I might not have taken over flying the airplane in the first place. With the engine shut down, this flight had just become something familiar and routine—just another glider lesson.

Letting Rob take over the flying may have been the natural thing for me to do, but I had another more practical reason for asking Rob to take the flight controls. The Mooney had become inexplicably nose heavy and I was struggling to keep the nose from dropping. His bigger biceps were advantageous right now. The explanation for why the airplane became nose heavy would be revealed days later, when the mechanics had their first chance to inspect the engine. The engine nearly fell onto the hangar floor because three of the four engine mounts had cracked all the way through. Even though we shut down the engine promptly when it seized up, the intense vibrations had nearly left us with an airplane that had literally "lost its engine." Without that weight in the front of the airplane, it would have been impossible to stay airborne.

Rob and I began planning our landing approach much like we did when flying gliders. Yet there were some major differences between the gliders and the Mooney. Gliders are designed to fly long distances without engine power, but the Mooney was going to descend much faster. The gliders we flew also had dive brakes which were like big boards that come out of each wing to allow us to slow down and increase the rate of descent quickly if needed. This allowed us to land in shorter distances and to descend steeply over obstacles like trees. The Mooney we were flying had no such devices (although later models added them because the Mooney was a challenge to slow down), but we had retractable landing gear and flaps that could be used to increase our rate of descent.

With the north-facing runway, runway 35, in sight, we knew we could make it to the runway—if we didn't mess up. We decided together when to put the gear and flaps down, and then Rob skillfully glided us to a smooth landing. Runway 35 at Manchester is over nine-thousand feet long, so instead of braking, Rob kept rolling, taking the first turn onto the taxiway, and then rolling us into a spot on the ramp just outside of a hanger. There were a few famous airshow performers who would shut down the engines of whatever they were flying at the end of their performance, glide in for a landing, and roll back into the same parking spot they had left from—it was like that, except with a dilapidated firetruck following us. We routinely practiced landing like this in the gliders so that we got off the runway without blocking it. Rob did even better than that because we didn't block the taxiway either. Rob was doing as he had been trained to do except in an airplane that he never expected he would need to do it in.

I was the first one out of the airplane because the only exit door was on my side. It was not a graceful exit. I slid off the wing, stumbling onto the ground, because slippery oil dripped off the back of the wing and tail. As I was standing there, my white sneakers soaking up the black oil, I could see more oil dripping like rainwater from underneath the entire length of the airplane. While I contemplated what had just happened, I overheard a conversation over the radio of the firetruck that was tuned to the tower frequency. I heard a male voice saying, "Wow, she didn't even block the runway. She was really calm on the radio too."

I let myself acknowledge that I had indeed remained calm, as had Rob. It was a satisfying feeling, matched only by the glee I felt when our tires touched the ground on our landing. That feeling didn't last long. Another male voice replied, "Yeah, but she was just in the *right* seat." *Really?* Besides the fact that flight instructors sit in the right seat, even if the person behind the voice assumed I was a passenger and not a pilot, did they think I was oblivious to the danger we had just faced? Was it so hard to believe a woman not only could be a flight instructor, but she could remain calm too in the event of an emergency?

As the four of us stood there watching the white airplane dripping black oil, I began to process the effect of the adrenaline pumping through my body. My right leg, but not my left, was shaking uncontrollably. I was self-conscious about it, hoping that no one saw it. My leg continued to tremble for several more hours as if it was disconnected from the rest of my body.

Two guys who worked at the airport pulled the Mooney, dripping like it had just come out of a carwash that used oil instead of soap and water, into the hangar where it would sit until a new engine could be installed. I didn't even ask if these guys had the authority to use this hangar. The plane had abandoned me, and I was now abandoning it. All I wanted to do was to get away from the scene before any reporters showed up. Like any responsible pilot, I kept going over the sequence of events in my head, wondering if I could have done anything better.

Rob's friend Jim, who had helped to calm my sister and was congratulating Rob on his landing, was solely concerned that I might get into trouble for allowing him to ride in the back. Despite my repeated assurances that it wasn't against the college's policy to take passengers on training flights, he offered to hitchhike home and pretend like he was never there. I was taken aback by his thoughtfulness. I knew Jim wanted to fly helicopters in the military. Based on what I had observed, he was the perfect candidate for flying those secret special operations we hear about only after they have resulted in the capture of some most wanted villain. I hope he got to do that.

I soon began thinking about how we would all get back to our home airport in Nashua while knowing that the college's only available airplane with more than two seats was the one hemorrhaging oil in the hangar. It would potentially take four of the college's smaller Cessna-152s, which only had room for a pilot and one passenger, to fly us home. Then I heard a familiar voice over the firetruck's radio that was still tuned to the tower frequency. An instructor who heard what happened had borrowed a Piper Cherokee and could fly three of us home, and he asked the tower to relay to us that he was on his way. That still left us needing one more seat, and again Jim offered to hitchhike home.

I had just finished telling Jim that I would wait for another instructor to come get me when a man approached us. I was afraid he might be a reporter but was relieved to find out that he was a pilot who owned a four-seat airplane. He heard everything that happened over the radio and wanted to help us get back to Nashua. I quickly decided that Sherry and Jim should fly home with him, and that Rob and I would wait for my friend in the Cherokee. I was still in the mode of an instructor, and I wanted to fly home with Rob in case he was ready to talk about what had just happened. I didn't want to pressure him, but I also knew it was important to debrief such an important event. After all, it was still a flying lesson.

Rob and I both climbed into the back seat of the Cherokee, neither one of us wanting to sit up front where we might be expected to fly or talk on the radio. We told ourselves that we were just tired from our ordeal, and we would have denied having any reservations about getting right back into another single-engine airplane. Yet when my friend pulled the power back to start our descent into Nashua, Rob and I involuntarily flinched at the sudden but expected decrease in power. While we were able to smile at our reaction, it showed that we were still in flight or fight mode.

Later that evening this same friend and his wife took Sherry and me out for pizza. It was then he reminded me that he, his wife, and I had flown in the same Mooney the night before from Nashua to T.F. Green International Airport in Providence, Rhode Island. We had flown over the densely populated suburbs south and west of Boston, where if the engine had failed it would have been nearly impossible to find a suitable place to land in the dark. It was a solemn reminder that, although experience and training can help prepare you for an emergency in an airplane, the outcome often involves some level of luck, or divine intervention, or whatever you want to call it, as well.

Since Rob had quickly disappeared back to his dorm after we landed, I decided to go track him down before I left for the weekend to make sure he was all right. I suspected that he and Jim might be enjoying an alcoholic beverage by then, and I was right. As I made the short walk from my office at the airport to the college dormitories, students from the college began clapping and cheering from their dorm windows when they saw me. I was touched by this gesture of support and surprised at how fast word had spread on campus about our emergency landing. A large percentage of the college's students were majoring in fields related to aviation, but even those that were studying other subjects had always embraced the aviation community on campus. Rob seemed to be in good spirits (no pun intended) and was surrounded by friends, so I headed out for the weekend.

By the following Monday, the story of our emergency landing had taken on a life of its own. Suddenly I was being asked what it was like to lose an engine while flying in the clouds, and then it became while flying in the clouds *at night*. And here I thought that our situation was harrowing enough already. It was like how the story of catching a small fish morphs into one about snagging a shark the more times it is told. It was embarrassing, but once again, there were two men who were ready to put me in my place. These two men were the mechanics who had completed a required hundred-hour inspection on the Mooney just before I had flown it to Providence. The Mooney had been flown for only three hours since their inspection when the engine quit. Even though they had not yet seen the condition of the engine, after I described the sequence of events leading to the engine failure, they did not hesitate to place the blame on me.

"Your student must have forgotten to tighten the dipstick (a device just like in a car where you can measure the amount of oil in the engine) and you must have missed it," they declared. I was incredulous, especially after I told them that I had checked the oil myself. Even after our successful landing, these two mechanics were trying to blame me for the engine failure. It made me wonder how insecure they felt about the work they had done on the airplane. I was willing to give them the benefit of a doubt until a cause could be determined for the failure. They were unwilling to do the same for me.

Many months later it was determined that our engine failure was caused by cracks in the crankcase—the housing around the engine's cylinders and connecting rods—that eventually became big enough that the entire oil supply was lost. With the engine now having no oil for lubrication, one of the connecting rods broke (the loud bang we heard) creating a large hole on the right side of the engine. The cracks were due to a manufacturing defect and were not something I could have detected since the airplane wasn't leaking oil before we took off. I also learned that other engines of the same type were discovered to have similar defects leading to engine failures both before and after our emergency landing. Some of those events resulted in fatalities. Eventually the FAA required additional inspections on those engines.

I had a few people who asked me if I was nervous to go flying in that Mooney after it got a new engine installed. The dean of the aviation division at the time made sure that I was the first one to fly this airplane after it got its new engine installed, and he flew it with me. Tom was a former Navy pilot who took off and landed on those compact floating runways on aircraft carriers. He was the one who had taught me and hundreds of other pilots how to do the thing we had just done—which was to say that he taught us how to always have an awareness of what we had to work with to get an airplane to operate at its maximum potential. Having an engine was one thing, but even with that engine not working we still knew we had altitude and speed that we could manage to allow us to glide as far as possible. I dare say that Tom and I had successfully taught this concept to Rob, with Tom using math and physics and with me applying it in the air with him. I am sure there are other instructors I worked with who also helped Rob to develop that skill and apply it when he needed it the most. It is no coincidence that one of Tom's students in his classes is a twelve-time, consecutive U.S. national aerobatic champion and premier airshow performer, and another earned a prestigious safety award for his skill at landing an airliner full of passengers after a serious problem with the flight controls. So, no, especially with Tom, who became my mentor and my friend, I was not nervous.

With the type of engine that was installed in the Mooney, it was recommended to fly it at a high-power setting for the first fifty hours. Tom and I flew circles high over the airport in Manchester for a while and then flew around just enjoying the view while monitoring the engine instruments for any signs of it running too hot. So, I wasn't apprehensive about flying it until one day I was scheduled to do a lesson in it where there were widespread low clouds. I knew the possibility of another engine failure in this airplane was extremely remote but flying it in the clouds and not being able to see the ground made me pause. I was pondering this as I waited on the phone for a briefing on the weather for our route that day. It was customary to give the weather briefer the registration number of the airplane we would be flying so there would be a record that we had received the required weather briefing. After I told the briefer we would be flying the airplane with the registration number of N801DW (pronounced November eight-zero-one-Delta-Whiskey in aviation jargon), he lowered his voice as if he was sharing a secret and said, "You might not want to fly that airplane. It had an engine failure recently."

Teaching Dad

The lights of the city below grew bigger, filling the window of the Cessna-150, as we slowly settled toward the ground. We seemed to hover for a moment, then we dropped like we had stepped into an elevator and found no floor beneath us. I was a new flight instructor, and the student pilot in the left seat, who had somehow gotten us into this precarious situation, was my father.

"Sorry, I didn't mean to do that," he yelled to be heard over the noise of the engine. We had no headsets or intercom in this barebones training aircraft, so all communication involved some level of yelling.

"It's ok, Dad," I yelled back as the high-pitched squeal of the stall warning horn reminded us that we were flying much too slowly and needed to lower the nose. We were on the precipice of an aerodynamic stall, where the angle between our flight path and our wing is too great and we were on the edge of being unable to keep our airplane in the air.

"That was my fault," my father said apologetically, even though we both knew that as his instructor I was the one who was supposed to keep us out of trouble. Dad was one of my first students after I earned my flight instructor certificate at the age of twenty, and my inexperience was evident in the vagueness of the instructions I had given him from the right seat. When Dad had initially failed to raise the nose of the airplane high enough for us to climb after we aborted our first attempt to land, I had directed him to "Get it up!" Instead, he reached for the first thing that could be moved up—the small gray lever that controlled the flaps. He flicked the flap lever up from forty degrees (full flaps down) to zero in one quick movement. The airplane responded predictably to the sudden loss of lift, and we teetered on the edge of flight.

"You didn't mean the flaps, did you?" he said with a tense smile as he lowered the nose, and we gradually started to regain our speed.

This is the event my father describes most often when asked what it was like being taught to fly by his daughter. He told me later that he really wanted to cuss when he made mistakes like that in front of me, but he kept it clean for my sake. For my part, I tolerated the triple checking of his seat belts, and his long-handwritten list of reminders to himself. Whenever I felt like I couldn't stand how long it was taking my meticulous father to accomplish a simple task, I reminded myself that without him I would never have considered the possibility that I could be a pilot.

My father had been interested in flying ever since he loaded rockets, bombs and torpedoes onto Douglas AD Skyraiders in the Marine Corps while stationed in Korea. This single engine, single pilot airplane was used for close air support when military operations needed to be conducted against hostile forces near friendly forces. The Skyraider carried its load of weapons on an external rack under the wings and loading the weapons while a Marine gave my father his first exposure to airplanes. He was new to this task of loading ordinance when, near the end of the Korean War, another Marine made a mistake loading a torpedo. The torpedo fired, zipping its way across the ramp lined with airplanes and soldiers. The Marine responsible for this mistake was supposed to leave for duty in Korea the next day, but my father was sent in his place instead.

Dad was nearsighted, and knew he could never fly for the Marines, but his fascination with airplanes was piqued by his time working on the flight line in Korea. He shared how he used to discuss flying and what it would be like to go into space with his best buddy, a guy with the unusual first name of "Story." Many years later, after my dad had started taking flying lessons with me, I realized while reading an article about NASA that the friend he had lost touch with was the astronaut Story Musgrave—the only astronaut to fly on all five space shuttles. Although my father was never going to into space like his buddy, I was happy to help him achieve his dream of flying. We made a pact that when it came to flying lessons, he was not my father but my student, and he would heed what I had to say. I agreed to not censor my comments to spare his feelings.

Some of those early lessons were made more challenging because my dad suffered from airsickness. We would be off the ground for no more than fifteen minutes before we had to head back with all the air vents blasting cold air in his face. Slowly things improved, and we were able to do lessons on days when the wind was blowing twenty knots or more. Dad never really liked the bumpy flights, but he had confidence in me and took every opportunity to gain more experience.

Dad talked to himself all the time while he was flying. If I wasn't giving him feedback, then he was critiquing himself—and he was much harder on himself than I was. Much like how people talk to their computers when things aren't going as planned, Dad also liked to talk to the airplane as if it were not an inanimate object. It often felt like I had to compete with his own inner voice and his constant cajoling of the airplane to fly right. A few years later I realized he was not alone in this habit. I had another student who was doing some solo practice when he mistakenly pushed and held the transmit button on his radio's microphone, known as a hot mic. He ended up broadcasting his cuss-filled admonitions to himself to everyone else on the frequency.

I'm sure it was a humbling experience for my dad to make all the typical mistakes of a student pilot in front of his daughter. He once started circling aimlessly during a lesson on navigation. When I asked him what he was doing, he said he was looking for the intersection of two tiny roads that he had highlighted in yellow on his neatly folded chart.

"Here's a thought, Dad. How about heading for that big lake up ahead instead?" We both laughed as he realized he could have flown toward the clearly visible body of water instead of searching for the intersection of two roads that was hidden by the plentiful trees that make up the New Hampshire landscape. I assured him he was not the first student pilot to attempt to navigate by the tiny things he imagined would be obvious from the cockpit of an airplane but were not.

Dad and I had few disagreements. One was on his first solo flight to another airport about fifty miles away from our home airport. I was relieved when he called on the phone to say he had landed safely, as we had discussed, but then he admitted he made an extra stop along the way. He had landed at an airport we had flown into several times together in Jaffrey, New Hampshire. There was an ice cream stand within walking distance of this airport and food was always a big factor when we were deciding where we were going to fly. It was not an airport I wanted him to fly into alone yet. The runway had a big dip in the middle which could make landings a bit tricky. When he realized that I was irate at his unauthorized landing (student pilots must have a signoff in their logbook from their instructor for each airport they are going to land at) he claimed he had landed there only to *confirm* it was the airport he thought it was.

"Well, Dad, that's a pretty lame excuse," I seethed into the phone. I reminded him the airport name was spelled out in big white letters on the taxiway that were readily visible from the air.

"Get back in that airplane and fly straight home without any more stops," I ordered. If he made any other detours, he kept them to himself, much like I had remained mum about some bad choices I had made as a new driver in his Ford Granada.

The only other time that things got heated between us was when he kept procrastinating about taking the required written test. After many months of taking practice tests, I finally told him I wouldn't fly with him again until he had taken and passed the test. He still has the piece of paper showing his grade of one hundred percent in a frame on his desk. I only got a ninety-five.

After Dad got his private pilot certificate, he managed to do one thing that I had never been able to accomplish; he got my mother to go flying with him. He bought an old Cessna-150 with a small inheritance he got from his parents. Every weekend the skies were clear and the wind was calm, he flew my mother over Lake Winnipesaukee while she napped in the seat beside him. I was offended by this since the one time I convinced my mother to go flying with me, she refused to look outside. She made me circle back for a landing as soon as we were off the ground and refused to go flying with me again.

The last time I flew with my father was on a visit home from North Carolina when I was six months pregnant with my first child. I took it as a good sign that the baby started kicking as soon as we applied full throttle, but within a few minutes I was overcome by morning sickness. I watched with amazement as my father expertly kept our airspeed up and quickly got us on the ground again.

While teaching my father how to fly had always been part of the deal for convincing my mother to let me take flying lessons, it wasn't the most memorable thing he did for me when it came to flying. The thing that stuck with me the most was his reaction when one of my first instructors made me circle a tree until I vomited and then told me that I would never be a pilot. As I sat defeated in the car on the way home that day, thinking that my father was going to tell me to quit taking flying lessons, my dad asked me if I wanted to keep flying. When I told him that I didn't want to quit, but I was afraid that this instructor was right, he said, "That is just one person's opinion who has just met you. Are you really going to let him have that kind of power over you?" I never forgot those words and I said the same thing to students when they were demoralized over a bad flying lesson or failing a checkride.

My father no longer flies as he approaches eighty-seven years old, but his enthusiasm for aviation has not waned. I gave him my collection of old flight manuals and he reads them repeatedly. His mind is as sharp as ever and I think his love of airplanes keeps him mentally engaged. When I no longer needed my leather flight bag to carry manuals that are now accessible on an iPad, I knew I couldn't just leave it collecting dust in a closet. I sent it to Dad.

One of the Guys

It was my first day at my job as a flight instructor at a New Hampshire college. I wanted this job so badly I spent hours on my cover letter and resume instead of studying for my college final exams. I remember typing out my cover letter on my well-worn electric typewriter, explaining to the chief flight instructor why I wanted to instruct for their aviation program. It was my dream job for that moment in life when all the possibilities are in front of you in a tantalizing but often intimidating way—where each choice seems like it will have a more profound impact than maybe it should.

There were seven full-time flight instructors on staff at the time, and one of the two female instructors was leaving for her first airline job. When the one remaining female instructor asked me to lunch, I envisioned sharing flying tales and teaching tips while bonding over our experiences as women in the male-dominated field of aviation. I remember sitting at a counter in a diner that specialized in subs and pizzas, waiting for our food, when Bianca grabbed a fistful of napkins and started talking.

"Let me tell you, they don't like female instructors here," Bianca said, referring to my new employer. "They don't give me students," she declared, "but the male instructors have lots of students." I was surprised, not because I was oblivious to sexism, but because it seemed inconsistent with what I had experienced during the hiring process. I worried if I had made a mistake coming here.

As Bianca talked more about her past, I learned that being a flight instructor was a second career for her. She had been a registered nurse working in a hospital prior to taking up flying, and she proudly shared how she and another nurse had once put a full body cast on an on-call resident who was sleeping. The story seemed implausible at best, and I began to suspect that something was amiss with my new colleague.

Bianca was petite, maybe five feet tall at the most, and tenacious but in a disorganized way. She spoke in a melodic voice that was at odds with her tendency to be abrupt in her mannerisms. I found it hard to imagine her being a soothing presence at anyone's bedside as a nurse, and it made me wonder what it would be like to fly with her. It would turn out that flying with her, not taking the job, was the mistake.

My priority in my new position was to get trained to fly the various airplanes that made up the college's fleet. Some of the airplanes, like the Cessna-152, were very familiar to me and I just needed to do one flight to be approved to teach students in it. The college also used motorized gliders like those used at the Air Force Academy. To teach in them I would need to learn how to fly and teach in them and pass a checkride. It was July and I was anxious to get trained before the new students arrived for the semester, so when my new boss said I should take a lesson with Bianca in the glider I didn't hesitate.

I had only flown the glider once before when I buckled in for my flight with Bianca. Once you are an instructor, the assumption is that you know how to teach, and so I mainly needed to learn the idiosyncrasies of flying something new. Bianca had just completed her training to become a glider instructor and had taken her checkride with my new boss. Given that I was an experienced pilot and instructor, I expected that she would give me some pointers while I got used to flying the glider. That was how my previous flight had gone, but that was not how Bianca did things.

One sign of an instructor who lacks confidence is they often keep their hands too tightly on the flight controls so that their student never gets a feel for how the airplane or glider flies. With Bianca, I sensed she was gripping the control stick for climbing, descending, or turning so tightly that she was undoing every correction I made. I was so sure she was not letting me do the flying that I slowly started to loosen my grip on the stick to see what happened. If I had been doing the flying without her intervention, then I would expect when I surreptitiously let go of the stick the glider would slowly drift off course. Instead, nothing happened. The glider stayed on its path as if it were on autopilot—which in a way it was, except Bianca was the autopilot. While I certainly understood the need to be vigilant when flying with someone for the first time, a good flight instructor knows how and when to intervene and doesn't secretly do all the flying themselves. Perhaps she just didn't trust me. I also had a hard time with Bianca's preferred teaching method which involved directing a nonstop stream of criticism at her students.

"No, not like that. No! Not that much! You're not getting it!"

On and on it went, this litany of negativity, without an ounce of constructive input on how I should be doing it instead. After my first landing, Bianca offered no critique except to say, "Watch me do the next landing," as if she was scolding a child. *You just did the last landing,* I thought, since she had not let go of the stick the whole time. I was miffed; even with student pilots who have never flown before, most instructors let them fly as much as possible and talk them through what to do. This was like deciding the best way to teach another driver how to handle a stick shift was to have them watch you shift gears.

As Bianca flew the glider in a rectangular pattern to set us up for her landing, I was surprised at how jerky she was on the stick, constantly adjusting the nose up and down instead of knowing where to put it to achieve the desired result in the first place. The glider required some eye-hand coordination when coming in for a landing because you had to use one hand to move the stick, and the other hand to adjust the dive brakes, panels that came out of each wing and helped to destroy lift for the landing. As Bianca struggled to coordinate her right hand on the dive brake handle and her left hand on the stick, the nose pitched up and down as if we were in a boat on rough seas, except the air was smooth.

After bouncing around the traffic pattern, feeling grateful that I was sitting on my blue boat cushion, I felt a jolt just before we touched down. Bianca had drifted off the side of the runway and the right main tire took out a runway light. Then Bianca let go of the stick with a loud sigh. Fortunately, I was used to salvaging bad landings when flying with new student pilots, and I managed to steer us back onto the runway and get us airborne again. As I climbed, Bianca said, "I think you get the idea. You can do the next one." *You bet I will*, I thought to myself, wondering how she had been approved to be an instructor in the glider in the first place. As soon as we landed, I saw that my boss, the same guy who had suggested that I fly with Bianca, had been watching from the ramp. He gave me a knowing and slightly guilty look, like he had no doubt that it was Bianca who took us on our meandering path off the runway.

"If you knew she was that bad, why did you tell me to fly with her?" I asked my boss. With all seriousness he replied, "I was hoping that you could teach her a thing or two." I seriously considered quitting my new job on the spot, but my last two instructing jobs had both ended abruptly when I was asked to do secretarial tasks like answering phones and typing for no pay while the male instructors flew with the students. I figured this job had to be better than that.

Although I managed to avoid flying with Bianca in the glider again, our paths soon crossed in other ways that shed light on why Bianca failed to have a cadre of successful students. I was waiting to take off on a busy summer day with a student, sitting on the taxiway that ran parallel to the one paved runway. There was a stretch of grass that ran alongside the paved runway that could be used to practice landing on soft surfaces (called soft-field landings). Landing on grass requires a technique that minimizes the rate of vertical descent by using some extra power and keeping the weight off the front nose wheel. This helps keep the tires from getting bogged down or stuck in the soft ground.

I saw Bianca and her student, Wes, on their final approach to the grass, but quickly realized they were going to touch down before the beginning of the grass landing strip. Although on a grass runway there are often no markings denoting the beginning of the landing surface like on a paved runway, it is usually obvious where the well-maintained surface begins. Apparently, this was not obvious to Bianca, or perhaps she was once again demonstrating for Wes and her landing technique was flawed. It was so obvious that Bianca was going to land short of the grass strip in the mucky, uneven mud that my student commented on it. "What are they doing? Don't they know the runway is over there?" he said, gesturing to the grass several hundred feet south of where they were headed. To make matters worse, the technique being used seemed to be a lesson in how not to land an airplane on soft grass. The nose wheel was pointed at the ground at such a steep angle it was going to plunge itself into the muck before the main wheels. There was a risk of flipping over if that happened.

I was thinking I should get on the radio and tell her to abort the landing, but someone else beat me to it. It did no good, of course, as Bianca was oblivious. As we sat there helpless, the airplane continued its steep path right into the mud. *Splat.* Fortunately, it didn't flip over, but the nose wheel was submerged below the surface with the airplane poised at a sixty-degree angle. Bianca and her student could be seen suspended by their shoulder harnesses in the cockpit, and Bianca was gesturing wildly to her student. I could only imagine she was telling Wes, "You see? Now you try the next one," as if nothing bad had happened. The airplane had to be pulled out of the mud, and Wes got the new instructor he deserved.

While it was clear to me what learning to fly from Bianca was like, I soon got to experience firsthand why her career in nursing may have faltered. One day while at work, I suddenly became violently ill in the women's bathroom. Bianca happened to be in the bathroom with me. That was a relief because I thought that I might pass out and no one would find me. That was a real possibility considering that other than Bianca, there was only one other woman in the building that day. Ironically, Bianca was examining herself in the mirror, commenting on how pale she looked while patting her cheeks, as I collapsed right beside her onto the floor. As my face hit the cool porcelain tile, I heard the door bump shut, and Bianca was gone. She hadn't noticed that I had fainted beside her, which might have been a clue as to why she struggled so much with flying. Knowing what is going on around you, also known as situational awareness, is an important skill for safe flying. Bianca seemed to have none of it.

I was finally discovered on the floor sometime later by the other female staff member who always knew what was going on and noticed I was missing. My boss got one of the bigger instructors to carry me to his truck, where he decided that Bianca should accompany us to the nearby emergency room because of her nursing background. I made a weak but impassioned protest against this idea since she didn't give me the warm and fuzzy feeling that I preferred in a nurse. It didn't work. Bianca rode in the seat beside me, where she now proceeded to slap my face every few seconds to keep me from closing my eyes as I tried to meditate to deal with the pain. When I mumbled that I was going to vomit, she unhelpfully told me that I wasn't while my boss drove the truck and simultaneously found a garbage bag in the glove department for me. I quickly proved that I was right. It turned out that I was diagnosed with a ruptured ovarian cyst and hospitalized for the night, but not before Bianca had loudly pronounced to everyone at the emergency room within earshot that I was just having menstrual cramps.

I did my best to avoid Bianca after that because it seemed like no good could come out of being around her, and she now seemed to see me as part of her problem being successful at this job. When she saw that I was progressing quickly through training and flying with students six days a week to keep up with the many advanced students I was now being assigned, she made some disparaging remarks about me being "one of the guys." I had heard rumblings that her job was in jeopardy. No one wanted to fly with her, and my experience ran contrary to Bianca's steadfast claim that sexism was at the root of her problems.

Several months later I was asked to do an evaluation flight with Bianca to assess her ability to fly solely by reference to the flight instruments like you must do when flying in the clouds. I would like to think that I was chosen for this task because I had more experience than most of the other instructors, but I suspected it was more than that. I am sure that the calculation was made that by having Bianca fly with me, the only other experienced female instructor on staff, she would not be able to cite gender discrimination as a reason for a poor outcome. I didn't want to acknowledge how strange it was that I was now evaluating the person who was supposed to be teaching me just a few months before. As I stepped into the cramped two-seat Cessna-152, I tried to erase the memory of that first flight with Bianca in the glider. To prevent Bianca from seeing outside once we got in the air, she wore a pair of oversized plastic glasses, called foggles, that allowed her to see only the flight instruments but not out the window—unless she sneaked a peak outside.

We were supposed to do some practice instrument approaches. This means that we were going to follow a chart which depicted a prescribed path to get lined up with the runway at a nearby airport. There are several different pieces of navigational equipment in the airplane that we could use for this. When I asked her to choose which approach she wanted to do first, she chose what was arguably the most challenging one to fly. She chose to do an NDB approach, like the one I had to do on my checkride a few years before with an engine out and half of my flight instruments covered up. I let Bianca use all the flight instruments and didn't give her any other malfunctions. My plan was to let her call the shots and just see how things turned out. With everyone I was teaching, I tried to set things up so that the flight would unfold naturally instead of concocting some situation that was unlikely to ever happen. This type of approach was challenging enough by itself.

In an NDB approach, a nondirectional beacon transmits a signal from the ground that is received by a piece of equipment in the airplane called an automatic direction finder (ADF). This piece of equipment is required because it shows the beacon's location relative to us on a round dial with a symbol that looks like a one-sided arrow. Unlike other methods of navigation which simply require a pilot to keep a needle centered to stay on course, the NDB approach requires you to calculate a path to the runway based on that arrow-shaped needle that moves every time you point the nose in a new direction. It's not intuitive in the least, and I have seen students do a complete circle trying to figure out what direction to fly to get lined up with the runway based on that maddeningly confusing arrow. Early in my training I was that student going in circles until I mastered how to do this approach properly.

Just the challenge of the approach made it an odd choice by Bianca, but what made it incomprehensible was that our airplane didn't have the required ADF equipment installed to detect the location of the beacon. There was just an empty hole in the middle of the instrument panel, approximately the size of a box of Pop Tarts, where this equipment should have been. It was hard to miss. It would be like if your GPS in your car kept telling you how many more miles you had to go but left out the instructions about how to get to your destination. I decided to see what happened next after she told the controller without hesitation that we wanted to do the NDB approach. It was a beautifully clear day, so I knew I could keep us from getting too far off course since I had done this approach many times before in good weather. I wanted to see how long she would fly around not knowing where she was going.

Initially the controller told us what direction to fly by giving us headings to set us up on course to intercept a path to the runway. I was astounded at how undisturbed Bianca was that there was nothing to look at to tell her where we were going relative to the runway. Normally the pilot puts the correct frequency into the ADF equipment and listens to the Morse code signal that confirms the correct NDB is tuned in. I thought she would notice there was no ADF equipment when she went to put the frequency into the box that wasn't there, but she seemed perfectly content to just fly around and not prepare for what came next. She could fly in the direction assigned by the controller for a while, but soon he would tell us to intercept the path to the runway and we would be on our own to figure how to get there. I silently watched, waiting for the moment she would have to acknowledge the empty space and realize she had nothing to navigate by to get to the runway.

Bianca was literally flying blind now with nothing telling her where the airport was, never mind the runway, and yet she made a turn to line us up perfectly with the centerline of the runway. It was then I knew she was sneaking glances out the window from beneath the foggles. I had enough of this charade, and I was livid but tried to hide it. The fact that she cheated didn't surprise me, in fact it was why I tried to fly with my students in bad weather so that they couldn't sneak a peek. It's tempting while in training to confirm you are on the right path, but when you are in a cloud you get no peeks. In a cloud you must trust your instruments. I was mad that she cheated so brazenly, thinking that I wouldn't notice we had nothing but a hole in the panel where the navigation equipment was supposed to be. Finally, I pointed to the hole in the instrument panel and asked with some sarcasm, "What are you using to navigate to the runway?'

"Oh," she said, obviously flustered, "I just knew it was time to turn." *Really*, I thought. *You must be psychic.*

I thanked the controller for his help and told him we would be returning to our home airport earlier than expected. Then Bianca and I flew home in silence. Neither of us said a word to each other, and although I usually helped students tie down the airplanes after we parked, I was so mad that I just fled inside as soon as the propeller stopped turning. I couldn't get out of the airplane fast enough. The chief flight instructor who had assigned me this task was waiting by the entrance to the flight operations building, anxious to hear how our flight had gone. He sensed from my demeanor that it had not gone well.

"Well, she chose to do an NDB approach," I said.

"Huh," he said, obviously surprised that she chose the most difficult of all the approaches. "How did that go?" he asked, not knowing there was missing equipment in our airplane.

"Not well," I said, "since there is no ADF equipment in that airplane."

That was the end of Bianca's job as a flight instructor at the college. I heard that she blamed me, telling everyone that I had given her an unfair evaluation because I was "one of the guys." What did that mean? Was a female pilot supposed to give another female pilot a pass no matter how unsafe they had become? Or had she experienced so much gender discrimination, or what she thought was gender discrimination, in her route to becoming a flight instructor, that she trusted no one to give her a fair evaluation? One thing I knew for sure is that she was in denial about her flying skills, and that the only safe place for her was on the ground. Or so I thought. Although I wasn't aware of it when I did my evaluation flight with her, Bianca had recently been involved in three car accidents that were all determined to be her fault. It appeared that Bianca needed a warning saying to use caution when operating all kinds of machinery and not just airplanes.

I lost track of Bianca after that until one day I received a newsletter from the local FAA office. When I saw her name, I thought that maybe she had been involved in another excursion off a runway or some such mishap, and that her story was being used as a cautionary tale for other pilots. Much to my dismay, Bianca was the recipient of an award for safety by the FAA. I could only hope that she had learned from all her prior mistakes and was now using them as teaching points to prevent others from following her path. The other possibility was too unbearable to consider—that she got this award because she wasn't, in fact, one of the guys, and that showcasing a female pilot was more important than showcasing a competent pilot.

Maybe this was how Bianca got here in the first place, where she thought that she had skills that she didn't have and was unwilling to accept feedback of any kind unless it was complimentary. Perhaps I had become more cynical since I had first started flying and was clueless about how much gender played a role in aviation even though an airplane is gender neutral—it performs the same way to the control inputs regardless of who is flying it. Still, it was perplexing to me how she got an award for safety until I talked to one of my best friends who worked in another region of the country for the FAA. When I told her this story, she explained that this award was for teaching safety seminars on the ground, but not for providing instruction in an airplane. In fact, it was likely that no one involved with this award had ever flown with Bianca.

I had to admit that I had also been featured in two newspaper articles about flying and the authors of those stories hadn't flown with me or talked to anyone who flew with me either. And I had been featured prominently in the marketing material for the college I worked at, even though no one who made that decision had ever flown with me. I was featured because I was female, just like a student who used to joke with me about how we were going to stay home the next time they did the photographs for the college catalogue. He was African American at a college and in a field that is overwhelmingly White, and we knew the photographers that followed us like Paparazzi were only trying to make our college look more diverse. I had to admit that I was sometimes part of this history of promoting aviators because of a diversity objective that had nothing to do with how we flew an airplane even if diversity was a worthwhile goal. The more I pondered what happened with

Bianca and my role in it, the more I felt as confused as she was as she tried to navigate to a runway with nothing but an empty space to guide her.

How Not to Fly an Airplane

Rain sizzled on the windshield as we were flung into a dark gray cloud. I was flying a Saab 340, a twin-engine propeller driven aircraft, from the right seat. I was the first officer for this flight. I knew we shouldn't be trying to fly around thunderstorms that were remnants of a hurricane that had recently passed through the area. I should have kept us on the ground. As if to reinforce my guilt, we were struck by lightning. And that was just the beginning.

I was twenty-six, with over two-thousand hours of flying in my logbook, when I was hired by a small regional airline based in Burlington, Vermont. The captain thought we could beat the line of thunderstorms, known as a squall line, between Hartford, Connecticut, and Albany, New York. I didn't think we should try. It was my job to convince him we should stay on the ground and wait out the storms.

"Are you sure you don't want to wait this out? It looks like it's moving fast, and the turbulence was pretty bad coming in here," I pleaded my case for not going.

"It's a short flight. I think we can beat it. If we can't we'll go around it, but it's worth a shot. OK, so it's your turn to fly this leg," he added. *Great,* I thought.

Prior to being hired by the airline, I had taught crew resource management to aspiring commercial pilots. Crew resource management or CRM involves teaching pilots how to effectively communicate and share the piloting duties on airliners that require two pilots. Crew resource management was required training at the airlines ever since a Lockheed L-1011 crashed into the Everglades with two pilots and a flight engineer at the controls in 1972. In that accident, no one was paying attention to flying the plane. All three pilots were so distracted with changing a light bulb for the landing gear indicator that no one noticed the autopilot had been disengaged. The airplane made a slow descent into the alligator-infested swamp.

A second accident in the Canary Islands five years later, the worst aviation disaster in history, reinforced the need for crew resource management training. A first officer failed to stop a captain from taking off even though he suspected another airplane was still on the runway. The two airplanes, both Boeing 747s, collided on the runway in the fog. Crew resource management training emphasized the need for first officers to communicate effectively to captains, and to collaborate on decisions on the flight deck. I had taught these concepts for the last four years but didn't apply them when it was needed the most.

When the lightning hit us, the two computer screens in front of me went black. They contained all the flight information such as our altitude and airspeed, as well as navigation information. I had to use a few small and awkwardly located backup instruments to fly the plane. Fortunately, the blackness lasted only a few seconds, and everything turned back on. Meanwhile, eight of the nine passengers, and the one flight attendant, were barfing in the cabin due to the severe turbulence—and probably because of fear. Turbulence can break an airplane apart in midair. The turbulence associated with thunderstorms is composed of strong updrafts and downdrafts, and rapidly changing wind conditions known as wind shear. It is as if a giant hand grasps your airplane and shakes it until pieces come off.

I could barely hear the captain over the pelting of the rain and the whacking of the windshield wipers as we taxied for takeoff. As we approached the runway, I realized that everyone else was waiting out the storms. The normally congested radio frequency was eerily quiet. The taxiways were empty except for the puddles and us. This was nuts. Sometimes the control tower would close the airport if the thunderstorms were close enough, but we were in the calm downpour before the storms arrived. Unfortunately for us, we were cleared for takeoff.

The first ten minutes after takeoff were bumpy but tolerable. Then with a jolt the turbulence escalated as we entered the dark, puffy clouds, bursting with rain. From the colorful radar screen, with its reds and yellows, and the greenish color of more clouds to the west, I knew we were not going to beat the squall line.

"Could you ask for a block altitude?" I yelled at the captain so he could hear me over the sound of rain pummeling us. A block altitude would give us a range of altitudes to fly. It was impossible to fly at just one altitude with the strong updrafts and downdrafts. The reply that came back over the radio from air traffic control was revealing.

"You're the only plane in the area. You can have any altitude you want." (*You idiots,* I could almost hear him thinking).

The empty sky was more evidence that no one was stupid enough to have taken to the skies in this weather. Meanwhile, the captain was fiddling with the radar screen, as if he tweaked it enough, the thunderstorms would go away. The flight attendant kept calling from the back for updates on when we would be in Albany. Most of our vomit-covered passengers knew this trip normally was over in thirty minutes. We had been thrashing around for an hour and a half.

Finally, the squall line moved through, and we broke out of the clouds in Albany. The rainbow the captain pointed out to the passengers probably did little to lift their spirits. I wondered if some of them might never want to fly again. One person who would not get back on an airplane was the flight attendant. She quit right there in Albany, taking a bus to wherever she called home.

On the way to the hotel, the captain conceded that maybe waiting out the storms would have been a better idea. I was so disappointed in myself that I nearly quit with the flight attendant that day. It was my job to advocate for the safest course of action. The captain was a congenial kind of guy. He probably would have been fine with staying on the ground, if only I had made my case more effectively. That was part of the problem.

It was easier to tell a jerk he was wrong than a nice guy. But my responsibility was to the passengers—not worrying about being well-liked. A lot of well-liked pilots were dead because no one wanted to tell them they were wrong. I vowed to do better the next time that bad weather threatened the safety of a flight, and I wouldn't have long to wait.

Pilots have always faced two seasonal adversaries in their quest to fly: the thunderstorms of summer, and the ice of winter. Ice forms in clouds or in precipitation when the temperature is below freezing. No matter what kind of airplane you are flying, if you want to keep it flying, you need to get out of the situation that is producing ice. Airplanes are not designed to fly with ice on their wings; ice adds weight and destroys lift, both at odds for defying gravity. To get out of the ice, pilots may have to climb, or descend, or get out of the clouds—whatever it takes. The trick is to know where there isn't any ice.

One of my colleagues, a first officer who was hired shortly after I was, had recently been killed in an accident due to ice. He had returned to our home airport of Burlington, Vermont from a four-day trip. It was snowing when he landed, and the snow was expected to continue throughout the night. Like many of our pilots, me included, this pilot didn't live in Burlington.

His home was in Albany, and after a trip he often caught a ride home with a cargo pilot who flew every night from Burlington to Albany. On this night he was late and landed just as the Cessna Grand Caravan, the largest single-engine turboprop on the market, was being loaded with the last of its cargo. I was told he literally ran from the Saab to the Grand Caravan parked a few yards away on the ramp. I imagine he must have been relieved to not have to wait until the next day to catch a flight home. In his haste on this dark night, he likely did not see the ice and snow building up on the wings. He also could not have known that the cargo pilot, in an added bit of irreverence for the weather and its power, had overloaded the airplane by one-thousand-one-hundred pounds.

On the takeoff run they were described as wobbling down Runway 15, struggling to get airborne. They crashed into the mountain ridge within five minutes of taking off. Both pilots died in the crash. Long after they were gone, my fellow aviator's footprints, where he had taken his last steps from the Saab to the Caravan, were still visible in the snow. They were a somber reminder of the hostile environment we flew in when the weather turned bad.

As spring arrived during my first year at the airline, I moved up in seniority and got the benefit of being able to fly more favorable schedules. This also meant that I found myself flying with the most senior captains at the airline. Some were eager to share their expertise with first officers. For others, their seniority was a sign that their decisions were never to be questioned. I had never flown with this captain before as we began a four-day trip.

On the third day of the trip, we were behind schedule due to the many things that can delay airplanes. We were supposed to end up in Ithaca, New York at eleven p.m., but it was after midnight, and we were still on a leg into Binghamton. The captain was close to the mandatory retirement age for airline pilots. He talked a lot about the past as I flew this leg, and as it got later, I noticed that he kept falling behind. He missed radio calls from air traffic control, forgot to call our company operations center to tell them we were inbound, and had to be reminded repeatedly to finish our required checklists. It was as if he was asleep with his eyes open.

When we landed in Binghamton, I was relieved to learn that fog had moved into Ithaca. The regulations dictated that for every runway the forecasted weather needed to show that we would have enough visibility to see the runway, or what are called landing minimums. Usually that meant that we needed a forecast that said we could see half a mile, but for some runways the requirements were higher for many reasons. For Ithaca the landing minimums were three-quarters of a mile. The fog had already moved in, and the forecast was for half a mile until sunrise. It was simple—we could not go and would have to spend the night in Binghamton. I was elated that we had to stay on the ground because I didn't think this captain was alert enough at this late hour to fly the leg into Ithaca.

Unfortunately, the captain was unaware that we needed more visibility, and the company dispatcher who provided us with the weather also missed the fact that we couldn't take off for Ithaca. Normally the dispatcher, who is responsible for flight planning and checking the weather, would have realized the weather was worse than landing minimums required and would have canceled the flight. But tonight, the dispatcher on duty was the only one I didn't trust, and for good reason. He had a reputation for making these kinds of mistakes, and the flight crews even called him "Skippy" behind his back because he was known to skip over some of his required tasks. It was also the case that most pilots who had flown these trips for as many years as my captain would have remembered that Ithaca had higher landing minimums—or at least would have looked at the chart to find out.

If we had taken off, we would have been in the precarious position of looking for the runway at night in fog. If we didn't see the runway, then we would have to abort the approach. This involved executing a fast-paced maneuver that required a lot of tasks to be completed in a short period of time. It was also something that rarely happened, and so the last time we had both done it was in our last training session. It was like throwing a fourth ball to a juggler that had only practiced with three for the last six months.

I don't know why I responded differently than I had in the past when we needed to stay on the ground. Whatever it was, I was not the same first officer who had ineffectively communicated with a captain in the past when he wanted to try to beat a line of thunderstorms.

"Call operations and tell them we can't go. We need three-quarters of a mile visibility and it's down to a half," I told the captain.

"No, we're good to go," he responded, clearly still not aware of the landing minimums for this airport, and in no mood to listen to me.

I repeated myself one more time, but he wasn't getting it. The next words out of my mouth shocked even me.

"I'm going to get the rental car and head to the hotel."

The flight attendant was standing next to me, looking bewildered at this conflict between the two pilots who were supposed to be working together.

I looked at her and said, "We can't go. I am going to the hotel. Care to join me?"

Without hesitation she said, "Yeah, I'm going with you."

The captain looked dismayed, but I now had his attention.

"We can't go. It's below minimums. We need three-quarters of a mile," I repeated, showing him the chart.

Still not satisfied, the captain called the company dispatcher again and confirmed that I was right. Not willing to give up his last semblance of authority, he returned from making the call to *explain* to me, "Yeah, you know we can't go. We don't have minimums. Let's go to the hotel."

As we walked to the rental car, he explained in detail why we couldn't go, as if it was his discovery in the first place. I didn't care. I just wanted to sleep peacefully that night, knowing that I had done my job. I had learned one of the most important lessons for a pilot—how to not fly.

He Was a Hero, She Was Calm

When I was sixteen, one of my flight instructors got hired for his first job at a small airline. Mark was in his twenties, the son of an airline pilot, and getting this job was a cause for celebration even though there was never any doubt that he would be an airline pilot. Mark was outgoing and friendly, always with a grin on his face. With his MG in British racing green and boyish looks, he was someone who might be a prime candidate for *The Bachelor* if he was not married at the time to the person who would be the first of his four wives.

I hoped to be in Mark's place someday (jobwise, not spousewise), and so I watched with some envy as he looked for a men's clothing store where he could purchase the items of clothing and accessories he needed for his new job. Some parts of Mark's new uniform, such as the epaulets, blazer, hat, and wings, were distributed by the airline. The rest, such as the black pants, shoes, and tie had to be purchased separately. There were several companies where you could order the white button-down shirts with the flaps on the shoulders for attaching epaulets.

About nine years later I was indeed in the same place as Mark, having been hired by my first airline, but my experience couldn't have been more different. I had trouble finding a company that made the white pilot shirts in women's sizes, and initially I had to order a men's shirt in the smallest size available. It was still so long that I struggled to tuck the shirttails into my pants, and when I did, it made me look a little bit like I had a diaper on because it was so bulky. Not the look I was going for.

I also had to shop in the men's department of a clothing store to find a black necktie, and I had no idea if neckties came in one size fits all, or small, medium, or large, or numerical sizes. Once I found one, I had to ask a fellow flight instructor to show me how to put it on correctly. Then I practiced tying it myself over the next few days as I prepared for my first trip as a first officer. I was so worried that I would forget how to do it that I kept it knotted around a chair in my hotel room each night of the four-day trip. While Mark had swagger in his new uniform, I felt like a disheveled imposter playing dress up in ill-fitting clothes. The whole experience did little to bolster my confidence as I showed up for my first day of ground school where I was the only woman in the class. While all the guys arranged to bunk with other pilots in this new city, I ended up sharing a room with a flight attendant who couldn't commiserate with me when I struggled to understand the electrical system on my new airplane.

While I may have felt like the world of aviation was unwelcoming to me compared to Mark, I knew that I was not alone in my experience. I can only imagine how the first female astronaut to fly on the space shuttle, Sally Ride, must have felt when she learned that the male engineers planning her mission anticipated she would need a supply of one-hundred tampons on board for the week-long trip. The brilliant minds behind the space shuttle apparently knew little about the opposite sex and were afraid to ask. Conquering space seemed doable, but women were still a mystery.

Even before I got hired by my first airline, I struggled with the masculine culture of aviation and what seemed like an impossible double standard when it came to things as trivial as the clothes I was supposed to wear. The president of the college where I was teaching told me that my choice of attire was important because it set the standard for our female flight students to follow. Despite being an avid watcher of the television show "What Not to Wear," I still felt ill equipped to be a fashion role model. While I understood the significance of a professional image for a college president, my situation was very different. I was the only professor at the college who had to attend faculty meetings and teach classes while also flight instructing in every airplane in our fleet. Figuring out what to wear for teaching and flying the college's aerobatic airplanes, the Mudry CAP10Bs, was especially challenging. I had to dress in a way that permitted me to put on a parachute and to be ready to use it. You don't want to be wearing your new pair of penny loafers and a pencil skirt while floating thousands of feet to the ground beneath the canopy of a parachute—especially not in the winter in New Hampshire. Male professors wore everything from blue jeans to three-piece suits and no one questioned the suitability of their attire.

While I was being singled out for my appearance, when it came to safety-related aspects of my job that uniquely affected me, I was being ignored. Most of the students I flew with in the CAP10 were men over two-hundred pounds who couldn't meet the weight limitations of the airplane with the other heavier instructors. I recall sitting through a long meeting where management discussed the newly revised policies for when an instructor and a student potentially had to jump from the airplane. They devised an emergency egress plan where the instructor was supposed to *throw their student out of the airplane* before jumping themselves. I was stunned as I pondered just how I was supposed to make this happen. The student who I was currently flying with weighed two-hundred-forty pounds to my one-hundred fifteen pounds. Three senior instructors, all men, explained how their method ensured that the student, who presumably might be frozen in fear, could be safely ejected out of the airplane. It was only after I asked how this was supposed to work for me and my big guy that any of them considered my situation. It was laughable that I would be able to throw my student anywhere. (I would also note that some of these same instructors were in no condition to be throwing anybody anywhere either, so I suspect this feat was more of a self-indulgent delusion than anything based on physics and math).

I admit that some of the angst I was feeling about my masculine work environment was exacerbated during this time because I developed romantic feelings for one of my colleagues. Although this instructor and I sometimes hung out together, it was clear that I was his platonic friend and that he wanted to go out with another one of our co-workers. Beth was not a pilot but instead worked in the office doing administrative tasks. While I arrived for work each day dressed for crawling under airplanes, Beth arrived in figure-flattering dresses and suits with coordinating accessories. She could have been a celebrity stylist if she had lived in Hollywood instead of New Hampshire. I was jealous of the attention directed her way by my crush who treated me more like a sibling.

I had worked hard to be accepted as a pilot and not a female pilot among my peers, and I had seemingly been *too* successful at it. While part of me didn't want the responsibility of representing female pilots and the added scrutiny this could bring, another part of me now resented the fact that I had felt the need to downplay my femininity because of it. Beth could arrive at work each morning looking like a model, while I was often dressed for a potential emergency landing in the woods. I had so wanted to be judged only on my skills and not my appearance, that I had stopped wearing nail polish after the chief pilot commented on how I was the only one who flew the college's airplanes with red fingernails. It hadn't mattered to me before, but now I resented the freedom that Beth and all my male colleagues had to be themselves while doing their job. I directed my feelings about the unfairness of the situation unfairly at Beth. I became envious of her, including how skillful she was at office tasks, while I still struggled to get the printer to use the right paper tray. It wasn't that I wanted to be more feminine to attract my crush's attention, it was the fact that he treated Beth and me so differently that forced me to acknowledge how much I felt like I had stifled a part of me.

It never occurred to me that Beth might feel like she was competing with me. Then one day I was typing a final exam for one of my classes when Beth walked by my office. "Geez," she said, "You fly airplanes, and you can type fast too? That's not fair." Why hadn't I considered that Beth might be feeling envious that I could fly airplanes? Later I thought of this encounter when I read the results of a study that had been done on how male pilots think about flying with female pilots versus male pilots. Many male pilots reported that flying with a female pilot was more relaxing because of the rampant competitiveness between male pilots. They expressed how nice it was to not constantly be thinking about how they were doing compared to their male colleague in the seat next to them.

I think that women working in masculine environments are sometimes drawn into similar competitive relationships with each other, often to the detriment of forming bonds that would otherwise mutually benefit them. In some ways it's not surprising this happens in aviation where women are often told that there are limited spots available for them. I was told by a large cargo airline that my resume wouldn't be considered because *enough* female pilots had already been hired that year—even though I had more flight experience than the male colleague that had just been hired. I was told a similar thing when I applied to fly for a corporate flight department where a friend had recently been hired. The chief pilot said they already had one female pilot and so there was *no reason* to even consider my qualifications for the other openings.

This is not to say that Beth was being treated fairly either. Even though she had a job that was commonly held by women, she was still working within the masculine culture of aviation. I slowly came to realize that some of the attention that came Beth's way was disrespectful and unwanted. There was an unfair assumption that someone with her looks couldn't be intelligent too.

The situation with Beth reminded me of the experience of another highly accomplished woman, barely in her early twenties, who came to take flying lessons at my home airport when I was a new flight instructor. Sarah confided that she had left her previous flight school because of issues with repeated sexual harassment. I was eager to fly with her, but a newly hired eighteen-year-old male instructor got assigned to be her instructor instead. As soon as Sarah's first lesson with him was finished and she was out the door, this instructor made an obscene gesture in front of me about the size of her breasts. I responded angrily to this, and he accused me of being jealous of her "physique." I felt protective of her, even though we were about the same age, and disgusted by the thought that my immature colleague might turn her off to flying for good. Sarah even confided in me one day that she was considering having breast reduction surgery partly to help with back pain, but also because she was tired of dealing with people who didn't take her seriously because of the size of her breasts. She soon stopped coming in for flying lessons, and I never saw her again even though I tried to reach out to her after overhearing her instructor bragging about making a pass at her during one of their lessons.

When I think about these experiences now, I can't help but observe that little has changed in the aviation industry more than three decades later. The percentage of professional pilots who are female has increased only a few percentage points since the 1980's. You need only look at the disparate experiences of two airline captains to understand how little has changed since Mark sauntered out of the dressing room in his new airline uniform and I struggled to figure out my new tie. The two pilots I am talking about are Sully Sullenberger and Tammie Jo Shultz. We all know who Sully is, but Schultz is not a household name. Schultz successfully landed her Boeing 737 after a sudden and violent engine failure that damaged the jet and resulted in a rapid depressurization and significant flight control issues. Not to take anything away from Sullenberger and his often forgotten first officer Jeffrey Skiles, but the situation Schultz faced was arguably more challenging.

Shultz had to contend with the painful effects of a loss of pressurization, and she had to communicate initially with her first officer using hand signals because of the intense noise. Schultz and her crew also had to contend with a smoke-filled, shuddering airplane that was missing chunks from the leading edge of a wing and the tail. Schultz didn't initially know what she was dealing with, unlike Sullenberger who could see the culprits that caused his engines to shut down automatically for him. (Thanks to the automated systems on the Airbus, Sully's engines shut down when the vibrations started. Shultz didn't have that on her Boeing). Schultz had an engine that failed in the worst way, flinging engine parts, which allowed part of a fan blade to break a window. She had to fly that damaged airplane with the knowledge that passengers and crew were attempting to save the life of a female passenger that was partially sucked out of that window.

Although Sullenberger and his crew faced the unenviable task of ditching in the Hudson, he was flying an Airbus that had been designed with some forethought given to the probability of a water landing; a ditching switch was installed to close some holes used for ventilation and pressurization so that it could be more airtight in the event of a ditching. Clearly Airbus thought that the A320 might not break apart when it hit the water. Schultz already had a sizable hole in her airplane, and the possibility that it would get worse. Sullenberger had a predictable airplane on his hands, albeit one that was now a glider. Schultz had to figure out how to keep her airplane from turning left now that the left engine was a hunk of debris.

Both pilots were rightfully commended for their skill and performance under pressure, but only Schultz had to fight for her right to be on the flight deck in the first place. Southwest Airlines fired Schultz, after her first year at the airline, based on a rumor about her past flying experience in the Navy that was untrue. Had she not been successful in suing Southwest to get her job back, her aviation career might have ended there. As it was, she still had to endure flying with a captain who poured coffee on the paperwork for each flight—making her fish it out of the trash on every leg they flew together for a month.

The fact that Sullenberger can often be seen making cameo appearances in movies and on television, says something about how we treat those who fit the stereotype of an airline captain. Even the words used to describe the two captains demonstrate the favoritism shown to Sullenberger versus Schultz. The news media used the term "hero" to describe Sullenberger, while stories about Schultz talked about how "calm" she was. *Gee, that sounds familiar.* Both pilots demonstrated professionalism, skill, and bravery under circumstances only a few pilots will ever face, but only the female pilot had to contend with the persistent stereotype that a woman will become overwhelmed by her emotions in life-threatening situations. Sullenberger was exalted for living up to the expectation that he would come through, while Schultz was applauded for defying the expectation that she would be hysterical. Sullenberger and Schultz both represent the best in aviation, yet only Schultz had to deal with those who may be the worst.

Before and After Pete

When I was twenty-four and still teaching for a college flight program one of my students was Pete. He had loved flying from an early age like I did. His childhood bedroom was full of the many model airplanes he had built hanging from the ceiling and filling every shelf. Even though he was only three years younger than me, he looked to me for advice about his flying career because I had completed his training for his commercial and flight instructor certificates. Those flights with Pete were some of the most fun I had flying with a student. Despite his easy-going personality that made him popular with his classmates, he was driven to build flight time quickly so he could get hired at a major airline at a young age. In a business where everything depends on seniority, he was keenly aware of how important it was to get hired as soon as possible, especially because the mandatory retirement age for airline pilots at that time was sixty.

Pete was also always up for a friendly competition. I remember doing a lesson with him in a glider on an unseasonably warm day in April, perfect for practicing how to stay aloft using rising pockets of air called thermals. Although clouds often provide visual evidence of where to find these cylindrical cones of updrafts called thermals, the art of circling in the center of one, thereby gaining thousands of feet of altitude, is based as much on instinct as technical skill. Pete had lots of both. Soon we were competing to see who could gain the most altitude in a thermal that rose off the black asphalt of a parking lot. I had tried circling to the right, and soon put us in a downdraft where we lost about a thousand feet of altitude quickly. Pete gave it a try, turning to the left. Soon he had pinpointed the spot where the upward momentum bumped us out of our seats, making us feel more like birds than pilots. It was flying at its most pure, and by the end of that lesson I felt like there was nothing left for me to teach Pete. It would be my last flight with him, and it would turn out that I still had important lessons that I had not conveyed well enough to save his life.

Pete had earned his flight instructor certificate as a means of building his flight time, but he was eager to fly airplanes with two engines because that was a requirement to get hired at a major airline. I don't think Pete enjoyed being a flight instructor although he took it seriously. He failed his flight instructor checkride on the first try, which was not unusual, but it was unthinkable for Pete. He was worried I would be mad at him, that he had let me down, because I had provided my recommendation for him to take the checkride. He was uncharacteristically emotional when he told me that he struggled on his checkride to explain how to fly a circle around a point on the ground while compensating for the wind. I suspected the maneuver was so intuitive to him that he couldn't grasp how to describe it.

One of Pete's best friends, Nate, was a student at the college who I had flown with a few times. Like Pete, Nate was a skillful pilot and eager to start acquiring the type of flying experience that would get him hired at an airline. I got to know Nate better when he started dating one of my first students at the college and one of the best pilots I had ever flown with, a pilot named Lily. It was an exciting time getting to watch these three and be part of the beginning of their journey as professional pilots. Nate had been hired to fly checks and newspapers at night for a cargo operation. It was a great gig in one way because all the flying was done in a Piper

Seneca, an airplane with two engines. I suspect Nate helped Pete get hired there too, and Pete was thrilled. I thought that Lily might one day follow in their footsteps.

Pete stopped by the classroom where I was teaching that summer before his senior year of college and asked if I could join him for lunch. He said that he had something that he wanted to get my advice about. It was a rare chance to get together because he was flying four or five nights in a row while also doing some flight instructing during the day. I wondered when he slept. We drove to a small café that still exists almost thirty years later just down the street from where I live. I have never been back there since that day with Pete.

He seemed uncomfortable bringing up whatever issue he was having and so I started asking him about the trips he was doing.

"It's great flying time," he said, like he was trying to sell himself on that idea. "I'm flying a lot," he said, then more hesitantly, "but I'm not sure about some of the things my boss expects me to do."

"What do you mean?" I pressed him between bites, thinking about some of the possibilities. It was well known in the industry that some unscrupulous freight operators pressured young pilots like Pete to fly poorly maintained airplanes in all kinds of weather. Knowing that aspiring airline pilots badly wanted the multi-engine flight time, they paid them little and threatened to fire them if they complained about their working conditions. They knew that aviation is an insular industry, where your next employer likely knows someone at your previous place of employment.

"Well, the chief pilot tells us not to do a runup before takeoff," said Pete, referring to when a pilot performs some checks on how the engine is running at specified power settings.

"Why wouldn't they want you to do a runup?" I asked, somewhat baffled since this is a normal procedure. The answer to this question revealed a lot about the mentality of the owner of the operation.

"They don't want you grounding an airplane, and if you don't look for a problem then you can't find one," Pete explained, summing up the rationale behind this directive from his boss.

"That's nuts," I said. "And anyway, that's an easy problem to fix. You just ignore your boss and do the runup anyway. If you find a problem, just tell him that the engine was running rough as you were taxiing, and he will never know the difference." It was typical of how I tended to solve problems, especially in those early years of my career, where I tried to find a way to solve an issue without being confrontational. I was always on "someone's radar" because I was a female pilot in a world full of male pilots, and I didn't need to attract any more attention my way.

Even as I said this, I knew there were probably more serious issues than what Pete was willing to tell me. This revelation from Pete about his boss probably only scratched the surface of unsafe practices this operation was engaged in. After thinking it over, Pete added, "I just want to quit. I know they don't maintain their airplanes like they should. And I'm so tired. I just want to go home for a couple of weeks and go golfing and eat some of my mother's cooking.'

It's here where I said something that still haunts me. Instead of telling Pete to quit, I said, "This is such a great opportunity for you to get multi-engine time. Only you can decide whether it's worth the risk." What was I thinking telling him this? I wanted to tell him to quit, but instead I acted like whatever he chose to do was inconsequential—like there were pros and cons to each choice when there was only one safe decision to make. I empathized with his plight when what he needed was for me to insist that his life wasn't worth this. If he was unconvinced, then I should have reminded him that if he was caught cutting corners, his pilot certificates could be suspended by the FAA, ending his chances to get hired by a major airline. In your early twenties you still tend to think that death is something that happens to others older than you. I should have talked to him about the very real threat to his future career—something that he could more easily grasp because that was where his head was at in his early twenties. The problem was that we were both in our early twenties.

Looking back on that day, I sometimes wonder if I avoided taking a stronger stand with Pete because of my own experience taking risks not that long ago in the pursuit of multi-engine time. When I was ready to get certified to fly multi-engine airplanes, my regular instructor reluctantly sent me to a nearby airport because he didn't have an airplane with two engines for me to fly. My new instructor, who was the same age as me at nineteen, was the son of the owner of the flight school. His demeanor while we were flying was lackadaisical one minute and terrified the next. He was not able to explain any of the maneuvers we were doing, and he often seemed to dread going flying. He also had a severe hearing impairment in his left ear, and since the old Piper Apache we were flying was very loud and had no intercom, we could barely communicate at all.

I knew something was amiss one day when my instructor was pacing anxiously when I arrived for our lesson. Without explaining our lesson plan on the ground, he started yelling after we took off about needing to shut down one of the engines. Normally, we would just simulate an engine failure by pulling back the throttle to idle on one of the engines, but today we were apparently going to do the real thing and shut the engine off. My previous instructor back home had told me we would do this to practice how to restart it in flight, but my current instructor wanted me to shut down an engine so that we could land with a perfectly good engine shut off—which really turned it into a "pilot induced" emergency.

To make the situation even a worse teaching moment, we were going to land back at the airport we took off from that had only one runway that was narrow and shorter than most runways. Part of practicing emergency procedures is to consider where the best airport is to divert to, and this airport was not it. If you have an engine failure, you should pick a long and wide runway if there is one nearby versus a short and narrow one, and if that airport has a firetruck or two ready to roll even better. The closest thing this airport had for a truck was an ice cream truck they used during the summer because it was near the beach.

I yelled back at him, having come up with a better idea, that we should either just restart the engine, or land at the airport with the nice long runways that was *right below us*. That's when he yelled, "No, we can't do that. My father says we have to do this!"

"Well, tell him we did then!" I yelled back, again coming up with a non-confrontational solution.

"We can't. My father will be watching."

Watching what, I thought? *The crash?*

This was the scariest thing I had experienced so far in an airplane. Not only did I not know what I was doing, but the person who was supposed to be teaching me was having something like performance anxiety, or worse. While I was occupied with trying to keep the airplane upright and figuring out when I should add the flaps and the gear, my "so called" instructor was completely checked out. There was silence to my right. But he had some awareness of the risk we were taking because he was shaking uncontrollably. All I remember thinking was *why are you here?* He would have been more useful on the ground because at least the airplane would fly better without his added weight.

Sure enough, by the time I landed about halfway down the runway, my instructor was hyperventilating, and his father was watching on the grass at the edge of the taxiway. I wasn't sure which thought scared me more—that his father insisted on us doing this dumb thing, or that he didn't trust his son, the one who was supposed to be training me, to help me do it successfully.

In the back of my mind that day at lunch with Pete, I was thinking who was I to lecture him about playing the odds in pursuit of multi-engine time? Instead of sharing my regret about doing something unsafe to get my first multi-engine time, and letting Pete learn from my mistake, I took the gutless way out. After our lunch, Pete decided that he was going to fly for this cargo operation for a few more weeks so he could get a little closer to accumulating the multi-engine time he needed to fly for United, Delta, or American Airlines. Then he was going to quit and take the rest of the summer off to golf and eat his mother's home cooking.

Two weeks later, on a Friday morning in June, I was following my usual routine of listening to a Boston area radio station while I was getting ready for work. The first story on the news that morning was about what was described as an "inferno" burning in a Dorchester neighborhood near Boston's Logan Airport. A plane carrying newspapers and bank checks had crashed into a triple decker house around one in the morning in heavy fog. The fire burned for hours, sending several people to the hospital for burns, and the lone pilot on the plane was dead. I knew Pete was scheduled to fly cargo that night, but I reasoned that it couldn't have been him. I knew he didn't have the required number of flight hours yet to be flying in that kind of weather and so I knew it couldn't be him. Yet somehow my body knew that it was. I was shaking uncontrollably, my body already processing what my mind couldn't accept.

I thought it was odd my body was reacting this way when I knew that Pete was home, in his bed in a room he rented in a house just down the street. It was the same room I had used a few times when I was in between apartments. I thought about calling the owner of the house, a friend of mine and Pete's, just to make sure he was there. I didn't because that seemed silly. It could not have been Pete. Just then I was startled by a knock at my door, even as I knew the news that was waiting for me on the other side.

I answered the door with my toothbrush still absent-mindedly in mouth. It was really Pete and not some nameless pilot on the news. I sobbed, first because I had never lost someone as close to me as Pete had been. It was later that I acknowledged the guilt of not stopping him from flying an airplane I knew had to have failed him. This was soon followed by anger at realizing that Pete had broken the rules by flying in poor weather when he didn't have the required training and experience. Even if in the end the crash was determined not to be his fault, I knew he would be blamed for not obeying the regulations. Why was he doing it? Was this what he had kept from me?

It occurred to me that the accident investigators would want to see Pete's logbook. A pilot's logbook is like an official journal of their flight experience. Each flight lesson they take is recorded on lined pages with room for a description of the flight including dates, locations, what airplane was flown, and whether any portion of the flight was flown in the clouds. I had recorded my last lesson with Pete in that logbook. It's like my fingerprints were everywhere.

Within an hour after hearing about Pete's death, I was able to retrieve his logbook. It looked like most pilot logbooks, a long rectangular book with a black vinyl cover and white, lined pages inside. It was the logbook of a pilot early in their career, before they usually purchased a larger version with many more pages.

I got a call that someone from the FAA was already looking for this logbook—my last connection to Pete. I was scared to open it and see what had transpired since our last flight together, but I felt compelled to see the truth. As I thumbed through the pages, trying not to let my tears smear the black ink on them, I realized he had documented all the ways he had violated the federal aviation regulations by flying for this company in bad weather. There was Pete's handwriting in black ink, documenting flights where he described dodging thunderstorms, flying in thick fog, and doing instrument approaches to airports where the clouds were so low he didn't know if he was going to be able to see the runway to land. It felt like a betrayal to hand over this incriminating evidence of his disregard for the rules knowing it would likely become the primary focus of the accident investigation.

Just as I feared, the accident was attributed to pilot error, and more specifically to a loss of control due to spatial disorientation. They were saying that just like in John F Kennedy, Jr's crash, Pete had lost his ability to know whether he was in a turn, or upside down, because he couldn't see the ground or the horizon. While it's true that pilots sometimes lose control of their airplanes due to spatial disorientation, the investigators dismissed evidence that a known mechanical problem with the forward baggage compartment door might have caused the crash. There was a long history of problems with the latching mechanism on this door which is located forward of the cockpit. Numerous incidents and four fatalities had occurred involving Piper Senecas after the baggage door opened in flight. According to the NTSB, in November of 1987, six months after Pete's crash, the FAA issued a requirement that certain inspections and repairs be done to the doors in response to these accidents.

There was also the fact that the company Pete was flying for had a long history of failing to perform required maintenance on its fleet of airplanes. The airplane Pete flew that night had numerous notations in its maintenance records of pilots reporting problems with the latching mechanism on the forward baggage door. There was no evidence that these problems had been fixed. There was also other evidence from the crash itself that pointed to potential mechanical problems. There was damage to the cockpit window consistent with it being hit by an object, and the forward baggage door was found at a different location than the rest of the airplane wreckage. Most disturbing, Pete's body provided a final devastating clue that something had come through the windshield causing a fatal blow to his head. Yet in the end the NTSB attributed the crash solely to spatial disorientation while noting that he was not qualified to do this flight. In other words, Pete broke the rules, and so he crashed.

Clearly, I had reasons to want the evidence to point to something outside of Pete's control as the cause for the crash. Still, I knew about spatial disorientation, having experienced it myself while flying in the clouds with students. While spatial disorientation can strike any pilot, especially one who was as tired as Pete undoubtedly was that night, it usually happens when a pilot is making turns or doing other maneuvers where the mechanisms in their inner ear that tell them where they are in space are disturbed. Pete was on the final approach, flying a straight path to the runway, and had completed the turns that would have most likely triggered disorientation. He was also established on his final descent, so the motion of changing his rate of descent had already happened. It's not the way that spatial disorientation usually happens. It happens in the way it did in Kennedy's accident, when he likely turned off the autopilot and began descending and turning to set up for landing. And Kennedy wasn't breaking any rules that night, and still it happened.

When an investigation of an accident reaches its final conclusions, the report will note two kinds of factors in a crash. There are causal factors, which are the ones that make a crash happen, and factors that contribute to a crash, like fatigue. I felt like my inability to convey to Pete that he should have quit the job was a contributing factor. I will always wonder whether I could have convinced him to quit if I had been more direct with him. I can tell myself it wouldn't have made a difference, but since he came to me for advice, why would I think he wouldn't act on what I said? I didn't have all the facts, but shouldn't I have asked more questions? These were the thoughts I was having when I turned on the evening news that night. I wasn't prepared to see the video of the body bag being pulled from the crash site. I wasn't ready to hear Pete's voice as he made his last radio transmission to the tower.

In the hours after the crash, I didn't want anyone outside of my aviation colleagues to know that I was Pete's last flight instructor. I lived in fear that a reporter would find out and try to ask me questions. That meant that I had to pretend not to care when I overheard the cashier at a convenience store discussing the accident with the customer in front of me. This store was across the street from the house where Pete rented a room, something this clerk could not have known, but it made it even worse.

"They shouldn't let twenty-one-year-olds fly airplanes into Boston," she said nonchalantly, like age was clearly the issue. In some ways I understood that kneejerk reaction from someone I assume was not a pilot. My impulse was to scream at her to stop talking about something she knew nothing about. Instead, I ran out the door, knowing my anger was misplaced. I was mad at myself, and unwilling to accept that a part of me was mad at Pete.

I would leave the job at the college three years later and move on to flying for a small regional airline. I was very picky about the companies I was willing to work for now, unlike how I had felt before Petie's accident when I jumped at any chance to get multi-engine time. Nate helped me get an interview for a job, and when I told him that I didn't like the chief pilot's attitude, he supported me when I said I wasn't going to take the job. Neither of us were willing to do anything for a job. Nate and Lily got married, and when Lily found herself working in an unsafe situation, she advocated for herself in a powerful way. I would like to think we all made better decisions because of Pete. And when I returned to working at the college as a professor of aeronautics, whenever I taught the senior level class that prepared commercial pilots for their first paying jobs, I told them about Pete. I said all the things I wished I had said to Pete to my captive audience of students, unwilling to let this opportunity slip away once again.

Who is Your Captain

When you are a first officer, one of the most important factors in how a trip will go is the captain. At smaller airlines or corporate flight departments, you might end up flying with the same captains repeatedly—which can be great fun or a nightmare. At a large airline, you will likely fly many trips with a captain that you have never met before. The reason the captain is so important is because they ultimately have the final say when it comes to the big decisions, and they set the tone for how things will go in the cockpit. That can be the difference between a captain that eats canned sardines in the small cockpit or one who does the preflight inspection in the snow for you because you did it last time and are still drying out from being covered in slush and de-icing fluid. Many times, especially at smaller airlines or on chartered flights, the captain will likely also be your dinner and lunch companion for the duration of the trip.

My favorite captains to fly with enjoyed finding great places to eat at our destinations and liked to do some sightseeing if we had a long layover. There was one captain I used to try to fly with when we had overnights in Ithaca, New York. He liked to go hiking at some of the state parks with cool rock formations and to eat at the Moosewood Restaurant there—a well-known vegetarian eatery whose cookbooks were some of the first I owned. Another captain knew the best places to get Italian food in Boston for cheap. We got a flat rate per day for food on overnights, so being able to find good food cheap was not only fun but a necessity—especially on a first officer's salary.

Sometimes it was just a matter of two personalities not meshing, but occasionally the situation with a particular captain was more problematic. I was proud of the fact that I could get along with just about anyone, but there was one captain that made me feel unsafe. For me, that captain was a guy with the nickname of "On Time Tom." He was an amiable guy who got his nickname because of his propensity to rush on every flight so he could get on the ground and engage in his passion—running. He was the classic type-A personality, and everyone joked that his predilection for running was to compensate for his other pastimes—smoking and drinking. (I should note that Tom never drank within twelve hours of a flight—which sometimes was one of the reasons he wanted to get on the ground quicker so he could have a beer before his time was up). Tom hated to be late. Even if there was no way to make up time in the air because of a delay on the ground, Tom was going to taxi fast and ask the controller for every shortcut he could get.

This was how I ended up in a confrontation with Tom on a humid ninety-five degree-day at Reagan National Airport. On this day our airplane was full. Both the air temperature and our heavy weight were going to greatly diminish our climb performance and increase the amount of runway we needed for takeoff. This was before iPads were in every cockpit, and all our performance charts showing how much runway we needed for takeoffs and landings were contained in thick, heavy, leather binders behind the seats. Tom, being in his usual hurry, accepted an offer from air traffic control to take off from a shorter runway so that we didn't have to taxi very far. While Tom hightailed it down the taxiway to the shorter runway, I was grappling with the heavy binder to see if this runway was long enough for our takeoff. It was not even close. I told Tom that we couldn't use this runway while gesturing to the thick volume on my lap. He smirked and continued taxiing toward the shorter runway.

At this point I could have given up, knowing that we probably had enough runway to get off without a problem given that there is a little wiggle room in all performance calculations. Yet I knew if something went wrong on this takeoff, we might not have enough runway to abort safely.

"We can't use this runway," I repeated to Tom, pointing to the place on the chart where it indicated how much runway we needed given our weight and the hot air temperature. Tom continued to ignore me, and we were quickly approaching the runway threshold for the shorter runway. I needed to stop him, but how? Then it came to me.

I pushed the tiny button on the yoke and said, "Ground Control, we're sorry, but we checked our calculations, and we need the longer runway."

Tom could do nothing now that I had put it out there for everyone to hear. The controller immediately cleared us to taxi to the longer runway, and I saw a hint of a smile on Tom's face, like he appreciated the fact that I figured out a way to go around him. I still wasn't happy with Tom. I wanted a partner in the airplane, not a competitor, and Tom was all about winning. I tried to avoid bidding trips with him after that, but just like how that boy in third grade who sat behind me pulling my pigtails had ended up behind me again in fourth grade, Tom kept showing up to fly trips with me.

A few months later my scheduled captain called in sick, and I ended up in yet another predicament of Tom's own making. We were sitting at the gate at JFK Airport this time during the evening rush hour when all the international flights were trying to depart. To cut down on the number of transmissions to ground control,

JFK had a procedure where all the outgoing flights were supposed to listen on the ground control frequency for the controller to call them with their taxi clearance. At other airports the procedure was to call the controller first and say you were ready to taxi, but here the policy was, "Don't call us, we'll call you."

Tom waited impatiently several minutes for the controller to call us, and then he ignored the procedure and called the controller anyway, stating that we were ready to taxi. This did not go well with the harried controller. The reply that came back was, "I said to wait for *me* to call *you*. You're at the back of the line now—number forty-two to taxi." I am not exaggerating. And with that we sat. This situation was intolerable for Tom, and therefore a nightmare for me. He was fidgeting and muttering, and then he suggested the controller might change his mind if I called him. "Use your *sexy* voice," he added. I rolled my eyes at him as I pondered the best course of action, and then I figured we had nothing to lose. I waited for a break in the nearly nonstop radio chatter, and I took my chance.

"Ground Control, I want to apologize for my captain. I promise he won't talk on the radio again, but for my sake can we please get our taxi clearance?" Tom gave me a dirty look, but it worked.

"Ok," the controller said, "but I am only doing this for *you*."

I had only one more flight with Tom. On this trip, as with so many others, as soon as our wheels left the runway Tom called for gear up, put the autopilot on, pushed his seat all the way back, and went to sleep. The problem was that this time it was his leg to fly. Although you can program the autopilot to fly hands off from takeoff to landing, you still must make sure it's doing what you expect it to do. You should treat it like a third pilot in the cockpit, and one that might be screwing up. There are also circumstances near the ground where controllers assign headings to keep airplanes from hitting each other, and this requires the pilot who is monitoring the autopilot to manually turn the knob that moves the heading "bug" to the new heading. It's not difficult, but it does require the pilot to be awake.

On this flight, we were cruising near Hartford, CT when we got an urgent sounding call from the controller. "Traffic, two o'clock, same altitude. I'm not talking to him. Do you see him?" I looked out the window ahead and to the right, but I couldn't find the other airplane.

"Traffic not in sight," I replied, so the controller gave us a new heading to fly to avoid the traffic. I anticipated that Tom would turn the heading bug to start making the turn since it was his leg to fly, but he was still fast asleep. Just then the controller snapped, "*Are you turning now?*" I quickly pushed the button to disengage the autopilot and turned steeply to the assigned heading, suddenly seeing the other airplane that was too close for comfort. Despite the blaring alarm from turning off the autopilot, the urgent voice on the radio, and the sudden turn, Tom was still asleep. I never flew with him again and that was all right with me.

Recently a Gulfstream, a twin-engine jet, went off the end of the runway at a South Carolina airport after landing way down the runway at a very high speed. The airplane was substantially damaged. The cockpit voice recorder revealed that the pilots told one of the passengers that they were in a race and were going to beat another airplane to the airport. They were recorded saying, "We know what we are doing right now, this is a race. This is NASCAR." When I read about this accident, I couldn't help but think of Tom.

My Second Engine Failure

Given that engine failures are rare, particularly with the jet engines that I was flying now at an airline, it might have seemed like my chances of having another engine failure were infinitesimal. Yet as a pilot you never think that way because a wise pilot prepares on every takeoff for the possibility of an engine failure. Pilots are pessimistic like that, but it's a good strategy as long as you don't scare your passenger like one of my students did. He was so animated about his takeoff briefing and the actions to take in the event of an engine failure he said a little too loudly, "*When* the engine fails after takeoff..."

One of the biggest causes of engine failures is fuel starvation (the engine quits because it's not getting fuel) and that is often, but not always, a pilot-induced problem. I was sure that this wasn't going to happen to me because I would never let the airplane run out of fuel. I know that it's hard to believe that someone would keep pushing on when they knew they were low on fuel, but I know of more than one pilot who ran out of fuel because he was trying to get to another airport where the fuel prices were cheaper. Flying is expensive, so you must be careful with your money after all.

Engines that fail due to fuel starvation also include the unfortunate situations where something prevents the fuel from getting to the engine. In one case a wasp nest in the fuel tank shifted on takeoff in a small Piper aircraft, causing it to block an air vent which created a vacuum in the tank. This prevented fuel from leaving the tank. In this case the engine quit while climbing out, and the pilot glided back to the airport for the mechanic to check it out. When the mechanic found nothing wrong, the pilot took off again and the same thing happened at the same spot. This time the mechanic drained the fuel tank and found the nest blocking the vent.

Engine failures due to fuel starvation also include situations where the fuel is contaminated with water. I once refueled a friend's Piper Cherokee before he flew at night to another airport. After going out to dinner, he returned to his airplane and took off. When he got only three-hundred feet in the air, the engine quit. He managed to land safely on another runway that didn't even have the runway lights on, but he knew that runway was there. Like I said, good pilots are always ready for an engine failure. It turned out that I unknowingly had filled his fuel tanks with fuel that was contaminated with water. The water had time to settle to the bottom of the tank during the time he was on the ground. He had checked for water contamination before the first takeoff, but not the second, not realizing it takes time for the fuel and water to separate out.

So given all the data on the most likely causes for an engine failure, I thought that the odds were slim that within three years of my first engine failure I would have a second one. And I never thought that a mechanic would be the *cause* of my next engine failure and that he would be literally breathing down my neck when it happened. I was a new first officer on the Saab 340 for a regional airline when I arrived for a four-day trip. Instead of meeting at the usual place, I was told to meet my captain at our maintenance hangar. One of our airplane's two engines had just had work done on it and they wanted us to fly it first to make sure the engine was now running properly before we loaded passengers. My feeling at the time was if there was so much uncertainty about the repairs the mechanics had made, then why was the airplane released to fly again?

The captain, who I had flown with before, was seemingly unflappable. I found him to be intimidating because he spoke very little and only about the task at hand. That is a good habit and a requirement when you are taxiing, taking off, landing, or below ten-thousand feet due to something called the sterile cockpit rule, but when it's the way someone behaves for an entire four-day trip it is unnerving. So, it surprised me to see that he was in an uncharacteristically animated discussion with the mechanic when I arrived. As I walked across the hangar, I could hear the captain telling the mechanic that he was coming with us on our flight. It was not unusual to take a mechanic along for a flight such as this, but this mechanic's vehement refusal to go was unusual. Sometimes mechanics only like to work on airplanes but not fly on them, but since we often had to fly our mechanics to other airports to fix airplanes, I didn't think fear of flying was his issue. His fear seemed to stem from the thought of flying on *this* airplane—the one that he had just worked on himself.

"You're coming with us," the captain repeated to the mechanic.

"No, I'm not," came the reply.

"Yes, you are," the captain said again, and I felt like I was watching a rerun of a fight I had with Ashley as a teenager when she didn't want to get out of bed on a Saturday morning to do anything but go for chocolate donuts.

I don't want to go either, I thought, but I decided to keep quiet.

Seeming to read my mind, the captain announced, "We are all going." The mechanic reluctantly buckled himself into the metal foldout jumpseat that was located just behind both of us in the cockpit. He also had a headset on so that he could hear our communications and could talk to us over the intercom. Now that I am past middle age, I can say with confidence that the mechanic's facial expression was much like the one I've seen on the faces of patients in the waiting area about to go in for their colonoscopies.

Everything went off without a hitch right up until the point when our wheels left the ground. Just as I announced, "positive rate" to the captain, indicating that we had started to climb and the signal for us to raise the landing gear, the mechanic said, "Oh, shit!" He had been leaning forward in the jumpseat, intently watching the engine instruments for the right engine, and he saw what was coming before it happened. Suddenly it was as if we had just turned off our right engine. There was a sudden decrease in engine noise followed by the dinging of bells that alert pilots that something is wrong, something like that dinging you get when you don't put your seatbelt on fast enough in your car.

I almost expected the captain to say, "I told you so." And so began the second engine failure of my flying career at the age of twenty-six. At least this airplane had two of them. The captain continued flying the airplane, so I started calling out the checklist items and let air traffic control know that we had an engine failure and were returning for a landing. Both the captain and the now silent and sullen mechanic wanted to get on the ground as quickly as possible. The problem was that since we were already at the airport, there was very little time to complete all the checklist items.

Sometimes pilots will circle around for a few minutes to complete everything on the checklist and to give the flight attendants time to prepare the passengers and the cabin. Since we only had the mechanic on board, there was no need for that, but this still didn't give me enough time to do everything. Many of the items on the engine failure checklist required me to move a metal guard that covered toggle switches on the overhead panel before I could turn the switches off—and there were a lot of them. Meanwhile I was communicating with the tower and answering all the questions that controllers must ask when a pilot declares an emergency: How many souls are on board? *Three angry ones.* How much fuel do you have? *Plenty.* What type of assistance do you need? *We need a new mechanic.* (OK, that is just what I wanted to say, especially that last one.)

    The captain could have helped me by talking to the tower, for instance, but he and the mechanic were too busy glaring at each other to offer me any assistance. Sometimes it makes sense to just get on the ground as quickly as possible in an emergency, but I had to wonder if the captain's actions that day were based on a level-headed assessment of the risk, or if he was just rushing me so he could get on the ground and slug the mechanic. I have no idea what his thinking was because he wasn't communicating with me other than to give me another task to complete. As it was, we nearly landed with the gear up because I hadn't reached the point in the checklist where you put the gear down before he was ready to land. A gear up landing might have delighted the mechanic because it would have taken the attention off him and his failure to fix the engine properly—if only briefly. After all, he didn't say a word about the gear still being up and he was sitting there with nothing to do but watch what was happening. We landed about three minutes after we took off. The captain and mechanic were still arguing when I made my escape down their stairs they brought over to the cabin door. My next thought was do I still have to go on a four-day trip with this now angry and sullen captain? *Yes, I did.* Who was going to have to fill out the incident report? *That was me too.*

She is a Pilot

I was a new first officer for a regional airline when I got the phone call I had been dreading. I was on standby as a backup pilot when the dispatcher put me on a four-day trip with Captain P. His reputation was well known among the female pilots. "He will start off by explaining how you should be home baking cookies and making babies," warned one of my female colleagues. Although I enjoy baking cookies and wanted to have babies, I also wanted to fly just like he did. Why couldn't I do all three?

As I settled into the right seat of the Saab 340, a twin-engine turboprop with thirty-four seats, Captain P started in with his views on the world. In his eyes, my place was not here in the cockpit but at home tracking my ovulation. Even when I told him I was eager to start a family after I became a captain, he still was not pleased I was his co-pilot for the next four days. Finally, we had something we agreed on. We started running through the checklists while I silently seethed in the right seat. I clung to the words of a fellow pilot who once told me that Captain P was fine to fly with once he saw that you knew your stuff. I felt like I was on trial and the judge to my left was already convinced of my guilt simply because I lacked a Y chromosome.

Unfortunately, it wasn't the first time that being a female in the male dominated world of aviation had become problematic for me. Once, I had been turned down for a job as a flight instructor because my flight training was done at my local airport rather than at a university with a large aeronautical degree program. My degree in business from the state university wasn't deemed to be good enough. I grew suspicious when I noticed a brochure on the front desk at the flight school that boasted, "It takes a tough man to make a great pilot." My suspicions of bigotry toward female pilots were confirmed when a male colleague applied for the same job that I had and was immediately hired. He had a fraction of the flight time I had, and he had not attended college at all.

During another interview for a job at a small airline, the chief pilot asked whether my husband approved of my flying, whether I wanted to have children, and whether my husband wanted me to get the job. He then asked me to fly a type of airplane that I had no experience flying—and not the type of airplane used by the airline—while justifying it by telling me that a female pilot he'd once hired had not "worked out."

Many male pilots also didn't make it through training, but he never made them demonstrate their flying skills before they were hired. I wanted to be treated just like the male pilots during the hiring process. Though I was offered the position, I declined the job offer. My job would have been to fly an airplane that required two pilots. For these airplanes, safety depends on both pilots being able to speak up when something is not going right. I knew this airline was not as safe as it should be if female pilots were not respected. I wanted no part of it.

So, when Captain P decided he would fly the first leg of the trip, and I would presumably sit in awe watching him, I was prepared for anything. I soon realized he was not a proficient pilot, despite his propensity to freely give advice to others. On the first leg of the trip, the autopilot failed, and we had to "hand fly" the rest of the day. This should not have been a problem for a proficient pilot, but Captain P's flying skills were subpar. He was one of those pilots who turned the autopilot on right after takeoff and left it on, so he didn't have to fly. It's not a good way to keep one's flying skills intact. I was in the unenviable position of being the one who had to point out when we were two hundred feet off on our altitude or flying in the wrong direction. He was not happy to listen to what he must have judged as "constant nagging" from the right seat, but that was my job. The non-flying pilot on each leg was responsible for pointing out any deviations from the proper flight path, so it could be corrected. I was pondering how long before Captain P tuned me out completely, or something worse, when it occurred to me what I needed to do.

"How about if I fly for the rest of the day?" I offered as earnestly as I could manage. "I can use the practice," I added, hoping he would not suspect my real intentions were to keep us safe by keeping him from flying. He leaped at my suggestion, so I flew the next three legs in relative peace and quiet except for a few "pointers" from the left seat. I eagerly anticipated getting an airplane with a functioning autopilot the next day, but suspected Captain P still preferred to leave me behind at the hotel.

The second day began like the first, with no camaraderie with my colleague in the left seat, but Captain P refrained from repeating his views on female pilots. I had just copied down our clearance from air traffic control when one of the gate agents asked if we would allow a passenger who was intoxicated to board. Allowing someone who is clearly drunk aboard would be a clear violation of the federal aviation regulations. We also knew that passengers who had a little too much to drink at the bar were boarded onto flights all the time, but this guy needed help just walking to the airplane.

"He's a happy drunk," the gate agent said, "and we think he will probably just fall asleep as soon as you take off." Captain P watched the "happy drunk" for some time as he considered his response (without conferring with me, of course). He decided he would allow the man to board and prepared to relay this message to the operations agent over the radio on the company frequency.

As Captain P pushed the button and started to transmit "Yeah, we will take the dru-," I noticed he was on the wrong frequency. He was talking to ground control, not company operations, so I quickly reached across to switch his frequency. He looked at me as if I had just ripped the captain's bars off his shirt. How dare I reach across to *his* side of the cockpit was the clear message.

"You were on ground control," I said hastily, hoping to avoid another conversation about my place in the cockpit. I will just go back to my little ole job over here, I thought, and keep you out of trouble.

"Thank you," he said, as he realized the potential consequences of his mistake. Making a public statement about his willingness to violate the regulations, and all on tape, was not a good career move to say the least. I had again made him look better than he was.

Soon, Captain P was telling everyone that I was a great pilot. He even offered to take my bags to the airplane on day three of our trip. I let him. The aviation industry being what it is, the airline we flew for was soon out of business, leaving both Captain P and me looking for other jobs. I lost track of Captain P but got a phone call one day from a friend of mine who was now flying as a captain for a small airline. He had flown as a first officer with Captain P and was my former roommate. He had listened to me rant about flying with Captain P, and his wife was also a pilot.

"You will never guess who my first officer is for my next trip. It's your old buddy Captain P," my friend said. Captain P had recently been hired to fly for this airline, so he was at the bottom of the seniority list and a first officer. My friend was now his captain because of hiring seniority, and he wondered if I thought he should give Captain P some payback for how he had treated the female pilots who flew with him. I suspect it was a long four-day trip for now First Officer P as my friend likely spent much of the trip bragging about his wife and all the other female pilots he knew and admired.

A few years later I realized that despite some of the challenges I faced as a female pilot, the fact that I was flying gave my daughter a different perspective on female aviators. At the age of nine, Christina went on her first airline flight to Denver to ski with friends. I was nervous since this was the first time she would be flying by herself, so I took her to my airline's training facility and showed her all the emergency exits on a Boeing 737. When she returned from her trip, she told me how the flight attendant tried to brief her on all the emergency exits on the Boeing 737.

"It was funny, Mom. I told her I knew where all the exits were because you had shown me. Then she said something weird. She asked if you were a flight attendant. Why would she ask that? I said no—she's a pilot!" To my daughter, I was a pilot, not a female pilot. Just as it should be.

Acknowledgments

This book would never have been published had it not been for four friends and former colleagues who insisted that I send the manuscript out. Thanks to Jennie Brown, Kathleen Fitzpatrick, Laurie Gordy, and Alexandria Peary. One of the first female pilots I ever met, Catherine Vuksanovic, has provided friendship and mentorship through everything I have experienced in the air and on the ground since the day we met at the airport when I was sixteen. I want to acknowledge my inspiring friend Jessica Webster who advocates for pilots who are caregivers at her nonprofit at Hera Aviation Group (heraaviationgroup.org). Thanks to Thomas Teller who has been a long-time mentor and friend to me and who I have had the pleasure of working with for so many years. Special thanks to my thesis advisor in the Master of Art in Science Writing at Johns Hopkins University, Kim O'Connell. I would like to also thank everyone at Apprentice House Press for making this book possible. I am grateful for all the pilots, flight attendants, controllers, and mechanics I have been fortunate to interact with for over forty years of flying. Last, but not least, special thanks to Dr. Timothy Gardner and Dr. Kerrington Smith who literally gave me my life back.

Prior Publications

The author gratefully acknowledges the publications in which several of these essays originally appeared: "How to Not to Fly an Airplane" in *The Atlantic*, "She's a Pilot" in *The Doctor T.J. Eckleburg Review*, "Teaching Dad" in *Air Facts Journal*, and "My First Day as a Professional Pilot" in *RavensPerch*.

About the Author

Shirley M. Phillips lives in southern New Hampshire so close to an airport she can critique all the landing approaches from her deck. She shares her home and her laptop keyboard with her cat, Amina. Her writing has been published in *The Atlantic, Dr. T.J. Eckleburg Review, RavensPerch*, and *Chicken Soup for the Soul: Lessons Learned from My Cat*, among other publications. More information can be found at her website at shirleymphillips.com.

Glossary

Autoland: A system that is part of an airplane's automation that allows it to fly an airplane's entire approach and landing, including the landing flare.

Block altitude: Permission given by air traffic control to operate an airplane within a range of altitudes. This can be useful when practicing maneuvers or whenever the pilot might want the ability to change altitude without requesting a new clearance.

Carburetors: Part of induction system of the engine where air and fuel is mixed and then delivered to the engine cylinders. Carburetors in an airplane can form ice in temperatures well above freezing. The signs of carburetor ice are a loss of power and engine roughness. Some airplanes are equipped with carburetor heat.

Checkride: The practical test that pilots must pass to receive their various pilot certificates like private pilot, commercial pilot, airline transport pilot, as well as their instrument rating that allows a pilot to fly in the clouds and low visibility. Checkrides are also required to fly certain airplanes like the Airbus or a Boeing 737,747,757, etc. The checkride consists of a flight portion and an oral portion where pilots must demonstrate a list of maneuvers in the airplane as well as answer questions about specified topics. Checkrides are administered by pilots that are designated by the FAA called designated pilot examiners.

Crew resource management (CRM): Crew resource management is a field of study that teaches a flight crew (pilots and flight attendants) how to work together efficiently and safely. A minimum amount of this training is required at U.S. air carriers and some other flight operators.

Flaps: These are surfaces that extend from the trailing edge of the wings that allow the airplane to generate more lift as a slower speed for takeoffs and landings. **Full flaps** are common for the final landing approach, and this means that the flaps are down to the greatest amount possible.

Flight protection systems: Computerized systems that prevent the pilot from overstressing the airplane or otherwise causing harm to the flight by limiting certain control movements or operation of certain systems depending on the flight condition of the airplane. These can include things like restricting the speed range of an airplane, limiting the bank angle, and limiting the angle of attack, among others.

Fly-by-wire (FBW): This is the type of flight control system where there are no mechanical linkages between the flight controls and their corresponding flight control surfaces. Instead, the pilot moves the elevators, rudders, and ailerons by sending an electrical signal to a computer which then moves the flight control surface via hydraulics. Although the controls in the cockpit can look like conventional systems, they function like switches that send an electrical signal. The F-16 has FBW, and the first commercial airliner with FBW was the Airbus A320 followed by the Boeing 777.

Foggles: A take on the idea of "goggles." Foggles are goggles used by pilots to restrict their vision out the windshield of their airplane. This allows pilots to practice, and be tested on, their ability to fly and navigate solely by reference to their instruments.

Fuel selector levers: These are levers in the cockpit that are used to open or close the supply of fuel from specific fuel tanks to the engine.

Hammerhead: A maneuver performed at airshows where the airplane goes straight up vertically until it can go up no more (because it would stall) then makes a U-shaped turn and comes straight down. To see the most innovative aerobatic maneuvers check out Rob Holland at https://www.ultimateairshows.com.

Heading: The direction that the nose is pointed in.

Heading bug: A small pointer on the instrument that shows heading information. It can be moved by rotating a small knob on the instrument. If the autopilot is engaged to maintain a heading, moving the "bug" turns the airplane to the new heading.

Heading indicator: A flight instrument that uses a gyro to provide information on what direction you are flying in degrees. For example, North is 360 degrees, South is 180 degrees, etc.

Horizontal stabilizer: The portion of the tail of an airplane that is horizontal, often fixed, and attached to the elevator. Horizontal stabilizers are designed to achieve the desired flying characteristics of an airplane.

NDB approach: An instrument approach that specifies what path to fly to get lined up with a specific runway or airport. Used for flying in the clouds and low visibility. This approach uses a radio signal from a beacon that transmits equally in all directions. Requires automatic direction-finding equipment (ADF) in the airplane to translate that signal into a relative direction from the beacon. It is being phased out in the U.S. but is still sometimes used in remote areas in other countries.

Landing flare: The part of landing an airplane where you lift the nose so that you make smooth contact with the runway and touch down on the main wheels versus the nosewheel.

Restricted airspace: A specified area in the sky where there are limitations on what aircraft can do there.

Side stick: This is used in the Airbus A320, some military aircraft like the F-16, and many business jets. It resembles a "joystick" and it is used by pilots for climbing, descending and turning.

Stall: An aerodynamic condition where the angle at which the airstream meets the wing, called the angle of attack, is too great. At this point there is a rapid loss of lift generated by the wing so that it can no longer produce enough lift to sustain flight. The angle of attack must be reduced to recover from a stall. A **spin** progresses from a stall when the wings are not equally stalled. It is a rotating, corkscrewing descent when the airplane has stalled. Stopping a spin requires you to recover from the stall.

Sterile cockpit rule: A federal aviation regulation that requires pilots to engage in only tasks essential to flying the airplane during critical times of the flight. This includes taxi, takeoff, initial climb, landing, and flight below ten-thousand feet unless in cruise flight only. This rule prohibits things like eating, non-essential communication, and reading.

Stick: The equipment in the cockpit used to climb, descend, and make turns that looks like a stick. These are more often used in older airplanes and those used for aerobatics.

Throttles/Thrust levers: A throttle is used to increase or decrease the amount of power to each engine in a propeller-driven airplane. Thrust levers are the equivalent device used to increase or decrease thrust in a jet.

Trim wheel: A device in the cockpit of an airplane used to relieve the pressure the pilot must apply to a control surface. For example, if a pilot is climbing, they will adjust the trim wheel so that they don't have to apply back pressure on the yoke or stick. The wheel moves a trim tab on the flight control that moves in the opposite direction of the control surface itself.

Turboprop: An airplane that uses one or more turbine engines to move a propeller(s).

Yoke: This is used to climb, descend, and turn in many airplanes and it's an elongated U-shaped control column that is centered in front of the pilot. It takes up more room than a stick or side stick.

Types of airplanes:

Airbus A320: The one-hundred fifty-seat airliner that was the first to use a fly-by-wire system. This is the same airplane that was ditched in the Hudson River by Sully Sullenburger.

Cessna-150/152: A high-wing two-seat training airplane with one engine, popular for training pilots.

Cessna-172: A high-wing four-seat airplane single-engine airplane that is one of the most popular airplanes ever built. It's used both for training and for recreational flying.

- **Cessna T303 Crusader:** A low-wing-six seat two-engine airplane with retractable landing gear that can fly up to 249 mph and fly as high as twenty-five thousand feet.
- **Douglas AD Skyraiders:** A single-seat support airplane used in both the Korean and Vietnam Wars to carry and use weapons located in a rack under its wings. It has a piston-engine and a propeller and was flying long into the jet age of military airplanes.
- **Grob 109B:** A two-seat motorized glider used for training pilots at the United States Air Force Academy and other places.
- **Mooney M20J:** A four-seat single-engine airplane named after its highest cruising speed of 201 mph.
- **Mundry CAP10B:** A two-seat airplane popular for training pilots in aerobatics. It was also used by the amazing aerobatic pilots who did performances all over the world as the French Connection.
- **Piper Apache:** A two-seat airplane popular for both business transportation and training pilots.
- **Piper Seminole:** A four-seat twin-engine airplane popular for training pilots in how to fly an airplane with two engines.
- **Saab SF340B:** A 34-seat twin-engine turboprop (a turbine engine driving propellers) popular before the development of small business jets.

Apprentice House Press
Loyola University Maryland

Apprentice House is the country's only campus-based, student-staffed book publishing company. Directed by professors and industry professionals, it is a nonprofit activity of the Communication Department at Loyola University Maryland.

Using state-of-the-art technology and an experiential learning model of education, Apprentice House publishes books in untraditional ways. This dual responsibility as publishers and educators creates an unprecedented collaborative environment among faculty and students, while teaching tomorrow's editors, designers, and marketers.

Eclectic and provocative, Apprentice House titles intend to entertain as well as spark dialogue on a variety of topics. Financial contributions to sustain the press's work are welcomed. Contributions are tax deductible to the fullest extent allowed by the IRS.

To learn more about Apprentice House books or to obtain submission guidelines, please visit www.apprenticehouse.com.

Apprentice House Press
Communication Department
Loyola University Maryland
4501 N. Charles Street
Baltimore, MD 21210
Ph: 410-617-5265
info@apprenticehouse.com • www.apprenticehouse.com